# THE
# RUGBY PANTRY

# THE
# RUGBY PANTRY
## HEALTHY MEASURES & GUILTY PLEASURES

**DAISY DAGG & AMBER VITO**
**PHOTOGRAPHS BY TAM WEST**

upstart press

A catalogue record for this book is available from the National Library of New Zealand

ISBN 978-1-927262-35-1

An Upstart Press Book
Published in 2015 by Upstart Press Ltd
B3, 72 Apollo Drive, Rosedale
Auckland, New Zealand

Text © Amber Vito & Daisy Dagg 2015
Photography © Tam West
The moral rights of the authors have been asserted.
Design and format © Upstart Press Ltd 2015

Designed by www.cvdgraphics.nz
Printed by Everbest Printing Co. Ltd., China

# CONTENTS

# INTRODUCTION

## WELCOME TO THE RUGBY PANTRY'S FIRST COOKBOOK!

We can hardly believe that this is the result of eating pizza in Rome together three years ago! Specifically, during the 2012 All Blacks end-of-year tour, we discovered that we shared a passion for travel and food. We spent two months travelling across Europe and Mexico together, enjoying all manner of culinary delights, from bangers and mash in London to fresh ceviche in Cancún. This was the beginning of our food journey.

After that amazing experience, we came up with the idea to do something of our own to share the joy of eating with others. A Facebook page was the answer and The Rugby Pantry was born. It was originally a simple way to share recipes with our family and friends, but it evolved very quickly into a popular site sharing recipes, tips and an insight into what All Blacks eat for health purposes and what treats they like to indulge in.

Our philosophy is that home cooking doesn't have to be complicated, time-consuming or scary, but meals should have great flavour, use fresh ingredients and be made with plenty of love. Our focus in this cookbook is presenting both healthy and naughty recipes that are easy to prepare. From guilty pleasures, such as nutella tarts, to healthy measures, such as quinoa salad, we like to mix up our recipes with easily accessible ingredients and great local produce.

There are so many dieting fads in today's society and many people seem too afraid to cook! In our cookbook, we disregard the all-too-common stance that most food is bad for you; we work on the idea that as long as we have everything in moderation, we can learn to cook and enjoy simple and delicious meals.

Because we are busy wives, mothers, and businesswomen we also understand the limited time most people have to cook family meals each night. So the recipes you'll find here are predominantly quick, easy, provide short-cuts and don't involve ingredients you can't pronounce. After all, we are home cooks, not chefs, who believe that Monday-night dinner can still taste great when prepped and cooked in 30 minutes or less.

Our husbands (All Blacks Israel Dagg and Victor Vito), who have very demanding jobs and equally commanding appetites, have personally sampled each of the recipes and given them the thumbs up. We've included a few of their favourites, some recipes passed down from our parents and siblings, and, of course, our own creations.

We hope you find as much pleasure in this book as we found in creating it.

## THANK YOU!

We would like to thank our agent Dean Hegan from Essentially Group, our publishers Warren Adler and Kevin Chapman from Upstart Press, and our lovely editor Jane Hingston. Thank you all for your unwavering support, and your faith in our abilities to produce this book. Your expertise is world class, and you have made this journey one we will never forget.

We would also like to thank our photographer Tamara West. Your unrivalled skill behind the lens has made our rustic meals present beautifully on paper. You were an absolute gem to work with!

A big shout out goes to our parents and families for our wonderful foodie upbringings. You have shown us the fundamentals of living off the land and sea, and fostered an appreciation for no-fuss cooking with great produce. From the beach to the bach, barbecues, and baking, this work celebrates you and all that is wonderful about Kiwi life.

Lastly, we would like to thank our amazing husbands, whose 'bottomless pit' stomachs and unwavering support gave rise to the creation of The Rugby Pantry. You are our inspirations and it's always a pleasure to cook for you!

Amber & Daisy

*Note: The initials at the end of each recipe indicate whether it was written by Amber or Daisy.*

# ABOUT THE AUTHORS

**AMBER VITO** grew up in rural Nelson. Her parents ran New Zealand's first gluten-free bakery, Dovedale Bread. Roland and Chrissie had travelled extensively, so she was very lucky to grow up in a family passionate about food from all cultures. A media graduate and wordsmith, Amber moved to Wellington to finish her postgrad study, which is where she met her husband Victor. Five years on they are happily married and have a five-month-old son, Karlos.

**DAISY DAGG** was brought up in Gisborne around the beach and the barbecue. She met her husband, current Crusader and All Black Israel Dagg, at high school and the two have lived in many locations since. Daisy has a degree in sports science, a diploma in interior design and owns a small interior business called Daisy Chain Interiors. She enjoys fishing, horse riding, travelling, playing sports and eating.

BREAKFAST
FOR
CHAMPIONS

# BLUEBERRY PANCAKES WITH CARAMELISED BANANA & MAPLE BACON

*Pancakes have got to be one of our favourite things to eat — and it was the first thing I learnt to cook at age eight! This recipe is simple to make and always turns out delicious.*

PREPARATION TIME: 5 MINUTES • COOKING TIME: 15 MINUTES • SERVES 4

1½ cups plain flour

3½ teaspoons baking powder

1 teaspoon salt

1 tablespoon white sugar

1¼ cups milk

3 tablespoons unsalted butter, melted

1 free-range egg

clarified butter (or coconut oil), for cooking

125g blueberries

250g streaky bacon (or 3 rashers per person)

4 tablespoons Canadian maple syrup

2 bananas

1 tablespoon brown sugar

dusting of cinnamon

Into a large bowl, sift the flour, baking powder, salt and sugar. Make a well in the centre and slowly add the milk, melted butter and egg. Whisk until smooth and pour into a jug.

Heat some butter or coconut oil in a frying pan on medium to high heat. Pour some pancake mixture into the hot pan and sprinkle 5–10 blueberries on top. Leave the pancake until small bubbles form and burst on the surface. Now it's time to flip. Cook for a minute on the other side, then transfer to a plate in a warm oven.

To cook the bacon, place rashers on a slotted oven tray which has tinfoil underneath. Turn the grill to high and grill the bacon for a few minutes on each side. Remove from the grill and brush the rashers with maple syrup before grilling for a further minute on each side.

Slice the bananas lengthways in their skins and sprinkle the cut-side with brown sugar and a little cinnamon. Fry the sliced bananas in butter or coconut oil on medium heat for 3–5 minutes until golden and caramelised. Arrange two or three pancakes on a plate and layer with maple syrup, bacon and bananas.

# BRIOCHE FRENCH TOAST WITH MANGO & HONEYED MASCARPONE

*This dish is so easy to make and was one of my favourites as a child. The smell of French toast often filled the Dallas household on a Sunday morning. The combination of mango and mascarpone is absolutely delicious.*

PREPARATION TIME: 10 MINUTES • COOKING TIME: 5 MINUTES • SERVES 4

125g mascarpone

½ cup cream

¼ cup runny honey

½ cup macadamia nuts

1 mango

4 free-range eggs, whisked

2 tablespoons milk

8 slices brioche (or other bread)

butter, for cooking

½ cup icing sugar

½ tablespoon ground cinnamon

Whip the mascarpone with the cream for about 20 seconds, until slightly fluffy. Drizzle the honey over and gently fold through so it marbles the cream.

Put the macadamias in a hot frying pan and toss gently until slightly coloured. Transfer to a bowl. Cut the cheeks off the mango, remove skin and cut into cubes.

Whisk the egg with the milk and place in a shallow bowl. Dip each slice of brioche in the egg mix, coating well. Heat a little butter in a frying pan on medium heat. Fry brioche until golden brown.

Sift the icing sugar and cinnamon over the cooked brioche and serve with a dollop of cream, mango, and some macadamias on top.

# EGGS BENNY WITH HOLLANDAISE SAUCE

*There are not many people in this world who don't like a good eggs benny! If you have time, have a go at making your own hollandaise sauce and serve on beautiful fresh bagels.*

PREPARATION TIME: 5 MINUTES • COOKING TIME: 10 MINUTES • SERVES 4

## HOLLANDAISE SAUCE

*2 free-range egg yolks, beaten*

*4 teaspoons water*

*3 teaspoons lemon juice*

*6 tablespoons butter*

*salt and pepper*

*¼ teaspoon cayenne pepper*

*¼ cup chopped fresh parsley*

*8 free-range eggs*

*8 rashers of streaky bacon*

*4 bagels, halved*

*1 avocado, sliced*

Combine egg yolks, water and lemon juice in a stainless steel bowl. Whisk together and add 1–2 tablespoons of the butter.

Make a 'double boiler' by placing the stainless steel mixing bowl over a pot of hot water on the stovetop. Stir continuously. The water should be hot and not quite boiling.

Continue adding the rest of the butter, a tablespoon at a time, while whisking vigorously. Add salt and pepper and cayenne pepper and continue whisking until hot and thickened.

Remove from the heat and add chopped parsley. If the hollandaise becomes too thick, add a teaspoon of warm water or lemon juice to taste. Set aside.

Pour boiling water into a frying pan. The water should be about 2cm deep. Slowly crack in eggs and swish water over the tops. Poach for about 2 minutes on low to medium heat or until eggs look cloudy on the top.

In another frying pan, allow bacon to sizzle for 4 minutes or until slightly browned. Pop bagel halves in toaster and cook until slightly browned. To serve, place two bagel halves on a plate, place avocado on each half, then bacon and poached eggs on top. Drizzle over the homemade hollandaise sauce.

# IZZY'S SALMON SCRAMBLE

*Scrambled eggs are a staple in the Kiwi diet and are so easy to make. Izzy always gets the Salmon Scramble at one of our favourite breakfast locations in Christchurch: Jagz at Styx Mill. As much as he loves the restaurant's Salmon Scramble, he decided to give it a go himself and became obsessed. You can put this meal on any type of bread, but there's nothing like toasted Vogel's!*

PREPARATION TIME: 5 MINUTES • COOKING TIME: 5 MINUTES • SERVES 2

6 large free-range eggs

¼ cup milk

1 spring onion

1 tomato

¼ red onion

100g smoked salmon

¼ cup grated Parmesan

salt and pepper

1 tablespoon butter

4 pieces Vogel's toast

4 teaspoons cream cheese

1 avocado, sliced

Crack the eggs into a large mixing bowl and lightly beat them with the milk. Finely slice the spring onion, dice the tomato and finely chop the red onion and add these to the egg mixture. Cut the smoked salmon into small pieces and add to the mixture along with the Parmesan. Stir thoroughly. Add some salt and pepper to taste.

Place butter in a non-stick frying pan on medium heat and let it melt. Don't allow the butter to brown or it will discolour the eggs. Pour in the egg mixture and let it sit, without stirring, for about 30 seconds.

Lift and fold the egg mixture over from the bottom of the pan. Let it sit for another 20 seconds, then fold again. Repeat until the eggs are set but slightly runny in places, then remove from the heat and let sit for another minute.

Pop the Vogel's in the toaster until browned. Spread a layer of cream cheese on the hot Vogel's toast, then place a scoop of scrambled eggs on top. Garnish with some slices of avocado and some more salt and pepper.

# MEXICAN BAKED EGGS

*Impress your loved ones or flatmates with this easy-to-make breakfast that looks as good as it tastes. We like to eat ours with fresh sliced avocado and toast for mopping up all the juice.*

PREPARATION TIME: 10 MINUTES • COOKING TIME: 20 MINUTES • SERVES 2 OR 4 SMALL PORTIONS

*1 tablespoon olive oil*

*1 small brown onion, diced*

*1 clove garlic, crushed*

*½ red chilli, de-seeded and finely sliced*

*½ red capsicum, diced*

*8 cherry tomatoes, sliced*

*½ a 400g can chopped tomatoes*

*½ a 400g can black beans*

*½ a 420g can baked beans*

*salt and pepper to taste*

*1 teaspoon smoked paprika*

*4 free-range eggs*

*½ cup grated cheese or crumbled feta*

*small handful of fresh coriander*

*1 ripe avocado*

*crusty bread*

Heat the olive oil, on medium heat, in a heavy-bottomed frying pan (that has a lid). Sauté the onion until juicy and tender, then add the garlic and chilli. Cook for another minute. Add the capsicum and cherry tomatoes. Turn the heat down to low and cook for a further 5 minutes.

Add the canned tomatoes and beans, season well with salt and pepper, then add the paprika. Stir to mix. Cook for 10 minutes, stirring occasionally.

Use a big spoon to make small indents in the top of the tomato and bean mixture and crack in the eggs as quickly as possible. Put the lid on and cook for 5 minutes if you like a runny yolk or 7 minutes if you prefer them more hard-boiled. Sprinkle with grated cheese, cover, and cook for a further minute (to melt the cheese). Garnish with chopped coriander and serve with slices of avocado and crusty bread.

# KOKO ARAISA (CHOCOLATE RICE)

*This Samoan favourite is Victor's requested breakfast treat when back after a long rugby trip. It's a cross between rice pudding and porridge, and has a rich almost smoky flavour. If you can't find koko Samoa, try using cacao nibs or good-quality ground cocoa.*

PREPARATION TIME: 10 MINUTES • COOKING TIME: 20 MINUTES • SERVES 4–6

2 cups medium-grain white rice

4 cups water

2 cups grated koko Samoa
   (or ground cacao nibs)

3 lemon leaves, quartered

300ml coconut cream (about
   ¾ of a 400ml can)

white sugar to taste

Wash the rice well until the water runs clear. Put it in a medium-sized pot with the water and bring to the boil. When it boils, add the koko and the lemon leaves.

Turn the heat to low and leave simmering for 5 minutes. Add the coconut cream and cook until it reaches the desired consistency. You can add extra hot water if you prefer a more soupy mix or leave as is for a thicker texture. Remove the lemon leaves from the pot and discard.

Add sugar to taste and serve hot in large bowls.

# SMOOTHIES

*All these smoothies can be made by simply mixing ingredients together in a blender.*

### BANANA & HONEY

*A great breakfast smoothie.*

1 banana

¾ cup almond milk

2 tablespoons honey

¼ cup plain unsweetened
   yoghurt

¼ teaspoon ground cinnamon

½ cup rolled oats

2 ice cubes

### BERRY BLEND

*A really healthy vitamin burst!*

¼ cup strawberries

¼ cup raspberries

¼ cup blueberries

1 banana

1 cup almond milk

¼ cup plain unsweetened
   yoghurt

2 ice cubes

### STRAWBERRY & MINT

*A refreshing summer slushy.*

6 strawberries, hulled

6 mint leaves

½ cup plain unsweetened
   yoghurt

½ cup coconut water

juice of ½ lemon

6 ice cubes

# TACKLING LUNCHES

# FRITTATA

*A dish with no bells or whistles, frittata tastes great and is perfect for using up leftovers. Make it for lunch or a simple healthy dinner. This version includes chorizo, gruyère and spinach, but frittata can be made with any leftover meats, veges and cheeses that you have in the fridge.*

## PREPARATION TIME: 10 MINUTES • COOKING TIME: 12–15 MINUTES • SERVES 4

*1 tablespoon olive oil*

*½ red onion, diced*

*100g chorizo sausage, sliced*

*2 cloves garlic, crushed*

*½ red capsicum, sliced*

*8 cherry tomatoes, halved*

*salt and pepper*

*1 teaspoon smoked paprika*

*6 free-range eggs*

*a splash of milk*

*handful of baby spinach leaves*

*½ zucchini, grated*

*small bunch of chopped parsley*

*½ cup grated gruyère or tasty cheese*

*4 slices Vogel's or crusty bread, toasted*

Set the grill to 220°C, with the rack in the upper half of the oven.

Heat olive oil in a heavy-bottomed ovenproof frying pan. Sauté the onion for a few minutes before adding the chorizo, garlic, capsicum and cherry tomatoes. Season well with salt and pepper and smoked paprika.

Cook for a few minutes on medium heat before spreading evenly across the pan. Beat the eggs with a splash of milk and a little salt and pepper. Pour the egg over the cooked ingredients and sprinkle in the spinach, zucchini and parsley. Cook on low to medium heat for up to 10 minutes, until cooked around the sides and just a little liquid on top. Sprinkle the cheese on top and season again.

Place the whole pan under the grill, leaving the oven door ajar. Let the frittata grill for about 5 minutes until puffy and golden on top. Serve hot wedges of the delicious frittata with Vogel's toast.

# FANCY BACON & EGG PIE

*With all our fishing trips and activities in summer, there's nothing like a good ole bacon and egg pie for lunch. Not a bad choice to warm you up on a cold winter's day, either. Whatever the season, there aren't many out there who don't enjoy this Kiwi favourite. Stray from the usual 'old classic' recipe and add whatever is in your fridge. It makes it lots more fun creating your own recipes!*

**PREPARATION TIME: 10 MINUTES • COOKING TIME: 45 MINUTES • SERVES 6–8**

*400–450g ready-rolled
    puff pastry*

*1 onion, finely sliced*

*1 tablespoon butter*

*1 tablespoon soy sauce*

*350g pack of bacon pieces or
    normal bacon*

*sprinkle of garlic salt*

*2 cups chopped spinach*

*2 tomatoes, chopped*

*¼ cup tomato sauce (plus more
    for serving)*

*50g feta*

*¼ cup fresh basil leaves,
    chopped*

*9 free-range eggs*

*½ cup milk*

*salt and pepper*

*1 cup grated cheese*

Preheat the oven to 180°C fanbake. Line the bottom and sides of a 2 litre baking dish with rolled-out puff pastry. Keep it fairly thick but, if too thick, roll out with a rolling pin for a thinner crust.

Place onion in a frying pan on medium heat with butter and soy sauce. Cook for about 4 minutes, until caramelised. Remove from the heat, cover and set aside. Cook bacon with garlic salt until browned, then add spinach and cook for another couple of minutes until spinach wilts.

Line the bottom of the pastry-lined baking dish with the caramelised onion, then add bacon and spinach mix. Add tomatoes and tomato sauce, then sprinkle over feta and basil.

In a small mixing bowl, lightly whisk together eggs, milk and salt and pepper. Pour mixture over the bacon and veges in baking dish.

Cut out another piece of puff pastry to place over the top of the pie. Squeeze pastry edges together, then sprinkle the top with cheese.

Bake for about 45 minutes. If the pie looks like it is browning too quickly, turn the oven down to 160°C and continue to cook.

Slice and serve with a good dollop of good Kiwi tomato sauce.

# CRISPY PRAWN TACOS

*For the past two years, Izzy and I have travelled to Mexico for a holiday. The first year we went to Cancún with Amber and Victor, the second year to Cabo San Lucas. It is one of our favourite countries in the world and the food is simply delish! On holiday in Cabo, we could not get enough of the soft-shelled tacos. They are fairly healthy and are a quick and simple lunch or light dinner.*

**PREPARATION TIME: 10 MINUTES • COOKING TIME: 5 MINUTES • SERVES 4**

*1 free-range egg*

*½ cup panko breadcrumbs*

*½ teaspoon garlic salt*

*1 teaspoon chicken salt*

*¼ cup olive oil*

*16 prawns, shells and tails removed*

*2 tomatoes, diced*

*¼ red onion, finely chopped*

*1 spring onion, finely sliced*

*1 tablespoon balsamic vinegar*

*salt and pepper*

*½ iceberg lettuce*

*2 avocadoes*

*8 small soft-shelled tacos or wraps*

## SAUCE

*4 tablespoons tomato sauce*

*4 tablespoons mayonnaise*

*1 teaspoon malt vinegar*

*1 teaspoon chilli oil or chilli sauce (if you want to add some heat)*

Whisk egg in a small mixing bowl. In another small bowl, mix the panko breadcrumbs, garlic salt and chicken salt together. Heat olive oil in a frying pan on medium to high heat. When oil is hot, dip prawns into egg mixture, then into breadcrumb mixture, then cook prawns in frying pan for about 30–45 seconds per side. Cover cooked prawns and set aside.

To make the salsa, place tomato, red onion and spring onion in a small bowl. Add balsamic vinegar, a dash of olive oil and salt and pepper to taste. Mix together.

Shred lettuce, slice avocado into lengths and set aside.

Remove soft tacos from packet and place in microwave for 30 seconds. Mix together all sauce ingredients in a small bowl.

To serve, place two warm tacos on a plate. Spoon a layer of sauce on the surface of each taco. Add lettuce, then salsa, and follow with prawns and avocado, stacking them in the middle nicely. Drizzle over sauce, then fold up the sides with fingers and *comer bien* (eat well)!

# STEAK & EGG SAMMY WITH BASIL PESTO SAUCE

*There is nothing quite like a good steak sammy to treat the taste buds. It is often a meal on a lunch menu at a café or restaurant, but they are so simple to make at home. The basil pesto sauce that goes with this sandwich adds a beautiful fresh fragrant flavour.*

**PREPARATION TIME: 5 MINUTES • COOKING TIME: 10 MINUTES • SERVES 4**

*1 onion, finely sliced*

*1 tablespoon butter*

*1 tablespoon soy sauce*

*4 free-range eggs*

*¼ cucumber*

*2 tomatoes*

*1 avocado*

*4 steaks*

*salt and pepper*

*olive oil*

*60g brie*

*fresh loaf of bread (tiger or ciabatta, preferably)*

*2 tablespoons mayonnaise*

*1 cup shredded lettuce*

*Basil Pesto Sauce (see page 180)*

Place onion in a frying pan on medium heat with butter and soy sauce. Cook for about 4 minutes until caramelised. Remove from heat and place in a covered bowl. In the same frying pan, fry the eggs, flipping after a few minutes so each egg is cooked on both sides (with the yolk remaining slightly oozy in the middle). Place on a covered plate to keep warm.

Slice the cucumber, tomatoes and avocado. Set aside.

Sprinkle the steaks with salt and pepper and place in the frying pan with a little olive oil. Cook each steak for 3 minutes on each side (for medium-rare). When nearly cooked, place two slices of brie on top of each steak. Remove from the heat and allow to rest for a few minutes.

Cut the loaf of bread into 2cm slices and lay out on four plates. Spread some mayo on the bread, then layer with the lettuce, cucumber and tomato. Place caramelised onion on top of the veges, then gently place the steak on top, followed by the egg and then the avocado slices. (Or any order you like!)

Drizzle the whole thing with the Basil Pesto Sauce and you will have yourself a mighty fine steak sammy.

# PULLED PORK SLIDERS

*Before trying pulled pork for the first time, I had always avoided it as I thought it would be a time waster. After cooking it, I discovered I was completely wrong. You basically just throw it in the slowcooker with a few herbs and spices and leave it to cook on its own. This is one of Izzy's favourite lunches and one I enjoy as the work is all done the night or morning before. Note you will need a slowcooker for this recipe.*

**PREPARATION TIME: 10 MINUTES • COOKING TIME: 8+ HOURS • SERVES 4**

*1 teaspoon ground cumin*

*1 tablespoon smoked paprika*

*1 tablespoon brown sugar*

*1 tablespoon mustard powder*

*salt and pepper*

*1kg pork shoulder roast (try to find one that will fit in your slowcooker)*

*½ cup apple cider vinegar*

*1½ cups water*

*2 tablespoons Worcestershire sauce*

*2 tablespoons tomato paste*

*1 tablespoon olive oil*

*¼ cup tomato sauce*

*¼ cup barbecue sauce*

*12 small slider buns*

*2 cups Homemade Slaw (see page 184)*

*1 avocado, sliced*

Make a dry rub by mixing together, on a plate, the cumin, smoked paprika, brown sugar, dry mustard and some salt and pepper. Place the pork on top and, with your hands, pat the dry rub onto every side of the pork. Place pork in the slowcooker with the apple cider vinegar, water, Worcestershire sauce, tomato paste and olive oil. Cook on low for 8 hours or overnight.

When cooked, remove from slowcooker and 'pull' the pork. It should pull away from the bone really easily. Place all the pork in a bowl and add ½ cup of the cooking liquid from the slowcooker along with the tomato and barbecue sauces. Mix together thoroughly.

Halve the slider buns. To serve, place pulled pork on the bottom half of a bun, followed by a heaped tablespoon of Homemade Slaw. Add some sliced avocado then top it off with the other half of the slider bun.

Serve 2–3 slider buns per person.

# SATAY CHICKEN BURGERS

*This burger is a delicious beast and could be made either for lunch or dinner. It is a great footy-night meal or easy to cook up on the barbecue or hot plate while camping. The secret ingredients to any burger are beetroot and avocado!*

**PREPARATION TIME: 10 MINUTES • COOKING TIME: 20 MINUTES • SERVES 6**

*2 onions, finely sliced*

*1 tablespoon butter*

*1 tablespoon soy sauce*

*2 tablespoons olive oil*

*6 boneless skinless chicken thigh cutlets*

*1 cup Satay Sauce (see page 180 or use shop-bought)*

*6 big burger buns*

*1 cup lettuce leaves*

*2 tomatoes, sliced*

*¼ cucumber, sliced*

*225g can sliced beetroot*

*2 avocadoes, sliced*

*6 tablespoons mayonnaise*

*salt and pepper*

Place onion in a frying pan on medium heat with butter and soy sauce. Cook for about 4 minutes, until caramelised. Remove from the heat, cover and set aside.

Heat some olive oil in a deep non-stick frying pan. Add the chicken thigh cutlets. Let brown for about 5 minutes on each side, then add the Satay Sauce and continue to simmer until completely cooked through. (This could take up to 15 minutes.) If Satay Sauce gets too gluggy, add water and continue to stir. When chicken is completely cooked through, remove from the heat.

Halve the burger buns. Place caramelised onion on the bottom half of each bun, then the chicken, lettuce, tomato, cucumber, beetroot and sliced avocado. Drizzle with some mayo, add a dash of salt and pepper and then slap on the top half of each burger bun.

# VIETNAMESE SPRING ROLLS

*These make a very healthy lunch. I often make them when I'm only making lunch for myself, as they are fast, simple, tasty and healthy. They are probably more of a girl's rather than a boy's lunch and are definitely suited to summer. You can use smoked or cooked chicken instead of prawns — or try them vegetarian.*

PREPARATION TIME: 10 MINUTES • COOKING TIME: 5 MINUTES • SERVES 4

*1 cup prawns*

*1 tablespoon sweet chilli sauce*

*1 tablespoon soy sauce*

*1 teaspoon crushed garlic*

*1 teaspoon olive oil*

*¼ cucumber*

*½ carrot*

*1 cup shredded iceberg or*
*   cos lettuce*

*½ cup fresh coriander and*
*   fresh mint*

*100g dried vermicelli noodles*

*8 round rice paper wrappers*

## DIPPING SAUCE

*juice of 1 lemon*

*1 tablespoon fish sauce*

*2 tablespoons sweet chilli sauce*

*½ fresh red chilli, de-seeded and*
*   finely chopped*

*2 teaspoons white sugar*

Place a non-stick frying pan on medium heat and add prawns, sweet chilli, soy sauce, garlic and olive oil. Cook for a couple of minutes, then cover and set aside to keep warm.

Chop the cucumber and carrot into matchsticks, and finely chop the fresh herbs. Place the vermicelli noodles in a bowl of boiling water and leave to sit for 5 minutes, then drain.

For each roll, dip a rice paper wrapper into a plate or flat bowl of warm water to soften. Place the softened rice paper flat on a board. Place some marinated prawns in the centre of the wrapper, followed by some vermicelli noodles, lettuce, veges, then herbs. Bring the bottom edge of the wrapper tightly up over the filling, and then fold the sides in over it. Continue to roll up tightly and place on a plate, join-side down.

Mix all dipping sauce ingredients together thoroughly in a small bowl. Serve two rolls on each plate with a small bowl of dipping sauce.

# VV'S PRE-MATCH EGG & HAM WHOLEMEAL PASTA

*This is Victor's favourite meal before a game: it has a good balance of protein and carbs for energy — and is pretty damn tasty too!*

PREPARATION TIME: 5 MINUTES • COOKING TIME: 20 MINUTES • SERVES 2

*sea salt*

*olive oil*

*250g wholemeal pasta*
  *(I use fusilli)*

*a little olive oil*

*6 free-range eggs*

*splash of cream or milk*

*salt and pepper*

*200g ham, shaved or sliced*

*handful of parsley (or sliced*
  *spring onion)*

*1 onion, diced*

*1 cup grated tasty cheese*

Boil about 4 cups of water with sea salt and a splash of olive oil added. Cook the pasta until al dente. Wholemeal pasta can take 15–18 minutes to cook as it is much denser than plain wheat pasta.

While the pasta is cooking, whisk the eggs with milk or cream and add salt and pepper before setting aside. Chop the shaved ham and parsley. Brown the onion in a frying pan with olive oil, over medium heat, until soft. Set aside.

Once the pasta is cooked, drain and return to cook on low heat. Add the egg mixture, parsley, onion, ham and cheese, stirring well. Stir for about 5 minutes, until the egg resembles scrambled egg, and the pasta is well coated. Season again and serve in a bowl with some extra grated cheese and parsley on top.

# PUTTANESCA PASTA WITH PROSCIUTTO

*My favourite country in the world, other than New Zealand of course, has to be Italy! I absolutely love their passion for food and their social occasions centred around food. I spent a lot of time there when I worked on a superyacht based in Sardinia. Drinking prosecco and eating puttanesca pasta were some of my greatest memories there. This recipe was inspired by Jamie Oliver's puttanesca recipe, but I have added my own touches. It is a great dish when cooking for a large group of people or when having an Italian-themed dinner party.*

**PREPARATION TIME: 10 MINUTES • COOKING TIME: 15 MINUTES • SERVES 6 (AS A MAIN MEAL)**

500g packet dried spaghetti

olive oil

sea salt and pepper

1 fresh red chilli, de-seeded and
    chopped

3 cloves garlic, crushed

15 pitted black olives

3 tablespoons capers

2 anchovy fillets, chopped

2 handfuls of Italian parsley,
    chopped (stalks and all)

juice of ½ lemon

800g jar of pomodori (or 400g
    can tomato pasta sauce +
    400g can crushed tomatoes)

¼ cup grated or shaved Parmesan

80g packet prosciutto ham,
    chopped

Bring a large pot of water to the boil. Add spaghetti, a dash of olive oil and some sea salt. Boil the pasta for about 10 minutes.

Heat a dash of olive oil in a wok or deep frying pan on medium heat. Cook chilli, garlic, olives, capers, anchovy, 1 handful of parsley, and lemon juice until slightly browned. Add the pomodori (or tomato pasta sauce and crushed tomatoes) and leave to simmer for 5 minutes. Add salt and pepper to taste.

Lift the cooked spaghetti out of the pot with tongs and add to the sauce. Twist the spaghetti through the sauce. If the pasta feels too gluggy add some of the boiled water until the mixture feels nice and light.

When sauce is spread throughout the pasta, serve immediately on a deep platter. Drizzle over some more olive oil and top with Parmesan, the remaining parsley, and prosciutto.

Best served straight away when hot.

Izzy and I absolutely love entertaining, barbecues and dinner parties. Often this involves cooking large amounts of food for the hungry rugby lads.

# ROASTED PUMPKIN SOUP

*Izzy only eats one kind of soup (pumpkin) and he loves it for lunch or an entrée. There are many soup recipes out there, but the roast flavours of this simple soup are delicious and warming. Serve hot with some freshly made garlic bread and you won't find much better on a cold winter's day.*

PREPARATION TIME: 10 MINUTES • COOKING TIME: 55 MINUTES • SERVES 4

*1kg buttercup (or other) pumpkin*

*2 potatoes*

*2 tablespoons olive oil*

*1 tablespoon garlic and herb salt*

*1 onion, finely sliced*

*2 cloves garlic, crushed*

*30g butter*

*2 cups chicken stock*

*1 cup milk*

*½ cup coconut cream*

*1 teaspoon salt*

*1 teaspoon pepper*

*4 rashers bacon*

*¼ cup Parmesan*

*5 leaves fresh basil, chopped*

Preheat the oven to 180°C.

Carefully slice the skin off the pumpkin and cut into medium-sized pieces. Peel the potatoes and cut into similar-sized pieces to the pumpkin. Drizzle with olive oil, season with garlic and herb salt and place in the oven to cook for 45 minutes.

Place the onion, garlic and butter in a non-stick frying pan and cook for about 5 minutes or until onion softens.

When pumpkin and potatoes are cooked, remove from the oven, cool a little, then put into a blender along with the onion and garlic mix. Add chicken stock, milk, coconut cream, and salt and pepper and blend until smooth.

Heat grill to 240°C. Grill bacon for 8 minutes or until brown and crispy. Remove from the grill and chop into small pieces.

Heat soup mixture in a pot on medium heat and cook for about 5 minutes, stirring often, until it is boiling hot.

To serve, ladle pumpkin soup into warmed deep bowls. Top each bowl with a heaped tablespoon of Parmesan and the crispy bacon bits. Finish with a sprinkling of basil.

# ROAST SALMON SALAD WITH MINT HONEY DRESSING & GARLIC CROSTINI

*It was an All Blacks test weekend in Wellington and Daisy was around for lunch. What better dish to make than a light and delicious salad? It's perfect for a warm day or a light supper with your friends.*

PREPARATION TIME: 15 MINUTES • COOKING TIME: 15 MINUTES • SERVES 4

## BAKED SALMON

*3 salmon fillets*

*salt and pepper*

*zest and juice of 2 lemons*

*good glug of olive oil*

*Mint Honey Dressing*

  *(see page 182)*

## SALAD

*2 navel oranges*

*1 small cucumber*

*2 avocadoes*

*120g bag of kale and spinach*

  *mix (or other salad greens)*

## CROSTINI

*4 cloves garlic, crushed*

*100g butter, softened*

*1 ciabatta loaf, sliced*

Preheat the oven to 150°C. Line a baking tray with tinfoil.

Place the salmon on the baking tray and season well. Using a grater, zest the lemon over the top of the fish. Squeeze on lemon juice and drizzle with olive oil. Bake for 10–15 minutes until flaky but still pink in the middle. (We like ours quite rare.) Set aside to cool slightly.

Peel the oranges and, using a sharp knife, cut into fine slices. Peel the cucumber and cut long ribbons using a peeler or a mandolin. Slice the avocado into wedges, seasoning well and squeezing over some lemon juice to stop browning. Toss orange, cucumber and avocado together in a bowl with the salad greens.

To make the crostini, preheat the grill to 220°C and line a tray with baking paper. Mix the garlic with the butter. Spread garlic butter onto sliced ciabatta and grill until crispy, about 2 minutes.

Once the salmon has cooled slightly, flake into the salad and pour over the Mint Honey Dressing. Serve with the crispy crostini.

# SEAFOOD SALAD

*This recipe is one I was taught by Izzy's family, the Daggs. I have added bits and pieces to it, as can you. It is a great salad when feeding a large group of people. Every Christmas I make this salad and it feeds a fair few. I often get asked for this recipe and it's almost embarrassing to tell people because it's so easy to make. But hey, when you're cooking for bulk, it's a winner!*

PREPARATION TIME: 10 MINUTES • COOKING TIME: 10 MINUTES • SERVES 10+

*500g packet shell pasta*

*olive oil*

*salt and pepper*

*½ red onion, chopped*

*2 tomatoes, diced*

*2 spring onions, chopped*

*1 cup chopped Italian parsley*

*500g surimi (frozen or fresh), chopped*

*300g small prawns or shrimps*

*Cajun seasoning*

*400ml bottle Thousand Island dressing*

*handful of chopped Italian parsley, to garnish*

Bring a large pot of water to the boil. Add the shell pasta with a dash of olive oil and a sprinkle of salt. Cook for about 10 minutes or until al dente.

Place red onion, tomato, spring onion, parsley and surimi in a large mixing bowl.

In a frying pan, cook prawns with a sprinkle of Cajun seasoning, olive oil and salt and pepper, until browned. Try not to overcook; they only take about 4 minutes on medium heat. When cooked, add the prawns to the mixing bowl.

When pasta is cooked, drain and rinse under cold water. Add warm pasta to the mixing bowl with Thousand Island dressing. Add some salt and pepper and mix until sauce spreads evenly through all ingredients.

Place in a large serving dish and sprinkle with Italian parsley.

# BIG RISONI & CHORIZO SALAD

*This amazing recipe is great for feeding large groups of people, and the bonus is that it is fairly healthy too. When I was asked to cook for 35 Crusaders I immediately thought of this salad, as it goes for miles! It is great for Christmas lunches and family barbecues and tastes superb.*

### PREPARATION TIME: 10 MINUTES • COOKING TIME: 15 MINUTES • SERVES 10+

*500g packet risoni pasta*
  *(or orzo)*
*a little olive oil*
*1 small red onion, sliced*
*250g sundried tomatoes*
*60g black pitted olives*
*1 cup chopped spinach*
*1 cup Italian parsley leaves*
*400g chorizo sticks (about 10)*
*salt and pepper*
*100g feta*

### DRESSING
*½ cup balsamic vinegar*
*juice of 2 lemons*
*2 tablespoons olive oil*
*salt and pepper*

Put the risoni plus a dash of olive oil into a pot of boiling water, ensuring the pasta is completely covered by the water, and cook for about 10 minutes. Stir occasionally to avoid the pasta sticking to the bottom of the pot. When cooked, drain and run warm water through it and set aside.

Slice the red onion and finely chop the sundried tomatoes, olives, spinach and parsley and place in a large mixing bowl.

Heat the chorizo on medium heat in a non-stick pot for about 5 minutes. Remove from the heat and allow to cool before cutting them up in pieces at slight angles. Add to the mixing bowl along with the drained risoni pasta. Mix together and add salt and pepper to taste.

For the dressing, in a small bowl mix together the balsamic vinegar, lemon juice and olive oil. Season with salt and pepper. Add dressing to the salad and toss to combine.

Place the salad on a big platter and, using your hands, crumble the feta over the top.

Can be served warm or cold.

# QUINOA & BACON SALAD

*Quinoa is a flavourful and nutritious grain that is easy to cook and provides a complete protein. It is the latest craze in the nutrition world so I thought I would try a few recipes. Here is a yummy healthy salad that is great for lunch or dinner.*

**PREPARATION TIME: 10 MINUTES • COOKING TIME: 10 MINUTES • SERVES 2 (AS A MAIN MEAL)**

*1 cup quinoa rice blend*

*2 cups chicken stock*

*¼ butternut pumpkin*

*8 rashers of streaky bacon*

*½ onion*

*1 zucchini*

*¼ eggplant*

*2 tablespoons olive oil*

*handful of spinach*

*1 teaspoon smoked paprika*

*salt and pepper*

*8 slices of halloumi cheese*

*½ avocado, diced*

For quinoa it's definitely best to follow the instructions on the back of the packet for measurements and cooking instructions, but I usually soak about 1 cup in water for about half an hour, then rinse and drain in a sieve.

Place the rinsed quinoa rice blend in a wok or deep frying pan with the chicken stock and cook on medium heat for about 15 minutes to reduce the liquid. If needed, add more chicken stock or water until the blend is thoroughly cooked through. Cover and set aside.

Skin the butternut pumpkin and cut into small pieces. Place in a microwave-proof bowl with a little boiling water and microwave for 3 minutes, or until it softens a little.

Chop bacon into small pieces and cook in a frying pan. Cut onion, zucchini and eggplant into small cubes and add to the frying pan. Add olive oil, spinach, smoked paprika and some salt and pepper to taste.

Put all ingredients together and mix through. Place in small serving bowls.

Fry halloumi in a separate frying pan. Place a slice on the top of each serving bowl with some diced avocado.

# CHICKEN & HALLOUMI SALAD

*This recipe is a quick and easy salad with crispy chicken and halloumi cheese. I often cook this when I feel like having a small meal, as it is a fairly nutritious lunch. You can add seeds and nuts or whatever seasonal veges are in your fridge.*

**PREPARATION TIME: 10 MINUTES • COOKING TIME: 10 MINUTES • SERVES 2 (AS A MAIN MEAL)**

*1 free-range egg*

*¼ cup panko breadcrumbs*

*1 tablespoon chicken salt*

*1 tablespoon garlic and herb salt*

*1 teaspoon smoked paprika*

*2 boneless, skinless chicken thigh cutlets*

*2 tablespoons olive oil*

*90g halloumi*

*2 cups mesclun lettuce*

*10 cherry tomatoes, halved*

*¼ cucumber, diced*

*1 zucchini, grated*

*2 tablespoons sunflower seeds (optional)*

*2 tablespoons chia seeds (optional)*

*1 avocado, sliced*

## DRESSING

*¼ cup ranch dressing*

*2 tablespoons balsamic vinegar*

In a small mixing bowl, beat the egg. In another small bowl, mix together the breadcrumbs, chicken salt, garlic and herb salt and smoked paprika. Cut the chicken into slices and add to the bowl with the beaten egg. Mix to ensure all chicken pieces are coated in egg.

Heat olive oil in a non-stick frying pan on medium heat. Using a pair of tongs, remove egg-coated chicken pieces, one at a time, and dip into breadcrumb mixture. Place in the frying pan and cook for about 5 minutes on each side, or until cooked through. When cooked, remove from the heat and place on a covered plate to keep warm.

Slice the halloumi and add to the frying pan. Cook for about 30 seconds on each side.

Divide the lettuce, tomatoes, cucumber and zucchini between two bowls. Add seeds or nuts (if using), then top with the cooked halloumi and crumbed chicken pieces. Garnish with the sliced avocado.

In a small bowl, mix together the ranch dressing and balsamic vinegar and drizzle dressing over the salads.

RUGBY
NIGHT
SNACKS

# ASIAN CHICKEN NIBBLES

*Make your own marinade in a jiffy and enjoy eating these yummy bites with your fingers!*

PREPARATION TIME: 10 MINUTES • COOKING TIME: 25–30 MINUTES,
AND 1+ HOUR FOR MARINATING • SERVES 4

## MARINADE

¾ cup dark soy sauce

½ cup sweet chilli sauce

2 cloves garlic, minced

1 teaspoon ginger paste (or a
   knob of fresh ginger, grated)

1 tablespoon sesame oil

good pinch of white pepper

½ red chilli, de-seeded and finely
   sliced

1 tablespoon runny honey

1kg chicken nibbles

2 teaspoons sesame oil

½ cup sesame seeds

1 spring onion, finely sliced

Preheat the oven to 180°C.

Mix all the marinade ingredients together in a large bowl and pour into a sealable bag. Seal the chicken in the bag with the marinade. Place in the fridge, ideally overnight but for at least 1 hour.

Using tongs, place the chicken in a tinfoil-lined roasting pan and drizzle over the sesame oil. Pour the leftover marinade into a bowl. Cook the nibbles for 25–30 minutes, turning at the halfway point and pouring any excess liquid out of the pan. Baste the chicken with the leftover marinade before returning to the oven. Once the nibbles are no longer pink in the middle, grill on high for 1–2 minutes each side to get a sticky, crispy skin.

Serve sprinkled with sesame seeds and spring onion.

# TERIYAKI BEEF LETTUCE CUPS

*These tasty cups are great to eat with your hands! The steak is tender and full of flavour when left to marinate for a few hours.*

PREPARATION TIME: 10 MINUTES • COOKING TIME: 6 MINUTES, AND 1+ HOUR MARINATING • SERVES 6

## MARINADE
½ cup Teriyaki Sauce
    (see page 181)
1 spring onion, chopped
knob of fresh ginger, grated
3 cloves garlic, crushed
ground black pepper

500g skirt steak
1 cos lettuce, middle leaves
    cleaned and removed
½ red onion, finely sliced
½ cucumber, peeled and cut into
    ribbons
garlic aïoli (or Kewpie
    mayonnaise)
½ red chilli, finely sliced
handful of coriander, chopped

Place the marinade ingredients into a sealable plastic bag and shake to mix. Add the steak, coating well in the marinade, and refrigerate for at least 1 hour and ideally overnight.

Cook the steak in a frying pan on medium to high heat for about 3 minutes each side, until medium-rare. Rest the steak for 5 minutes before slicing against the grain.

Place the steak in the lettuce leaves with the onion and cucumber, and top with aïoli, chilli and coriander.

# SCALLOP CROSTINI WITH CAPER MAYO

*We are so spoilt in New Zealand with some of the world's best seafood. This simple scallop recipe makes sure they remain the hero, but with a bit of added crunch and tang.*

**PREPARATION TIME: 10 MINUTES • COOKING TIME: 25 MINUTES, CROSTINI INCLUDED • SERVES 3**

## CROSTINI

*stick of French bread, thinly
    sliced*
*glug of olive oil*
*pinch of rock salt*

*2 tablespoons clarified butter*
*1 tablespoon canola oil*
*1 dozen scallops, cleaned but
    with roe left on*
*salt and white pepper*
*Caper Mayonnaise
    (see page 181)*
*small handful of fresh dill,
    chopped*
*1 lemon, sliced into wedges*

Preheat the oven to 180°C.

Line a baking tray with baking paper. Arrange rows of French bread on the baking tray. Brush each side with a little olive oil, sprinkle with salt and bake for about 6 minutes each side or until golden. Remove from the oven and leave to cool on the tray.

Heat a frying pan on medium to high heat. Add the clarified butter and oil. Pat down the scallops with a paper towel to remove any moisture. When the oil and butter have almost reached smoking point, add the scallops, six at a time (don't overcrowd the pan; the scallops shouldn't touch). Cook for about 1½ minutes each side and only turn them once. Place scallops on a warmed plate and season with salt and white pepper.

Assemble by placing a scallop on each crostini. Add a dollop of caper mayo and a sprinkling of dill. Serve with lemon wedges.

# GREEN CURRY MUSSELS

*I made up this recipe about five years ago when I was trying to re-create Lone Star's mussel recipe. I just wanted something similar, so decided to try them with a green curry and creamy garlic sauce. They actually turned out delicious, and I often use this as an entrée or starter when guests come over for a dinner party.*

PREPARATION TIME: 5 MINUTES • COOKING TIME: 10 MINUTES • SERVES 6

1kg green-lipped mussels
50g butter
4 cloves garlic, finely sliced
1 onion, finely sliced
2 tablespoons green curry paste
2 x 400ml cans coconut cream
slices of garlic bread

Place the mussels in a large bowl and discard any that are open and do not close when tapped.

Place the butter, garlic and onion in a large pot on medium heat. Fry until the butter is melted and the onion and garlic have browned. Add the curry paste and cook for another minute, then add the coconut cream. Mix and heat until boiling.

Add the mussels and cook until the shells all open. This should take around 5 minutes. Discard any mussels that do not open.

Leave the mussels in their shells and place in small serving bowls with the sauce. Place a couple of pieces of garlic bread on the side to scoop up the sauce when the mussels have been devoured.

# RICE BUBBLE PRAWNS

*These are a really yummy snack and super-easy to make. Perfect to serve in front of the big screen during the footy.*

PREPARATION TIME: 5 MINUTES • COOKING TIME: 5 MINUTES • SERVES 4

*2 cups rice bubbles*

*4 tablespoons plain flour*

*¼ cup water*

*1 teaspoon garlic salt*

*1 teaspoon Cajun seasoning*

*1 cup vegetable oil*

*15 king or large prawns,*
   *shells removed and de-veined*

*juice of ½ lemon*

*salt and pepper*

*½ cup Kewpie mayonnaise*

Place the rice bubbles in a small bowl. In another small bowl, mix the flour, water, garlic salt and Cajun seasoning to make a batter. (You are aiming for a fairly thick, heavy pancake-like batter that coats the prawns well. If it's too thick add some water, if too runny add more flour.)

Heat the oil in a frying pan to deep-fry. (Use a deep fryer if you have one.)

Dip each prawn in the batter, and then in rice bubbles. Cook for 30 seconds each side in the hot oil. If the rice bubbles start getting wet in the bowl, replace with a fresh batch.

When all the prawns are cooked, place on a serving plate. Drizzle over lemon juice and sprinkle with salt and pepper.

Serve with a dipping bowl of mayo (we like Kewpie the best).

# SALMON & AVOCADO TARTARE

*After an incredible week-long honeymoon in Bora Bora, Tahiti, Izzy and I became obsessed with raw fish dishes. Over there we ate stack-loads of raw mahi and tuna in salads, tartares and ceviche. This wee ripper is an adapted salmon and avocado stacked tartare. It is simply delicious and can be eaten either as a starter or a full meal — it is surprisingly filling. Note you'll need a ring mould for this recipe.*

**PREPARATION TIME: 10 MINUTES • SERVES 4**

## SALMON LAYER

*500g salmon fillets*

*1 tablespoon soy sauce*

*juice of 1 lemon*

*juice of 1 lime*

*2 tablespoons olive oil*

*2 tablespoons coconut cream*

*2 tablespoons chopped red onion*

*½ red chilli, de-seeded and
    chopped*

*chives, chopped*

*salt and pepper to taste*

## AVOCADO LAYER

*3 avocadoes*

*2 tablespoons mayonnaise*

*1 drop wasabi sauce*

*salt and pepper to taste*

*dash of olive oil*

*sesame and chia seeds (optional)*

*lime wedges, to garnish*

*freshly ground black pepper*

Skin the salmon fillets and cut into lengths and then small cubes. Mix the soy sauce, lemon juice, lime juice, olive oil, coconut cream, red onion, chilli, chives and salt and pepper together in a bowl. Leave to sit for 5 minutes while you make the avocado mixture, to allow the lemon and lime juice to soak into the salmon.

Cut the avocado into small cubes and add the mayonnaise, wasabi and salt and pepper. Add olive oil and mix gently. Mix in the sesame or chia seeds (if using).

Set the ring mould on a plate. Add a few scoops of the salmon mixture and pat down. Then add a few scoops of the avocado mixture and pat down. Remove the ring mould and you should have a nice little salmon and avocado tartare tower.

Add a lime wedge and some freshly ground black pepper.

# SUNDRIED TOMATO SALMON

*Nathan Tamihana, a salmon-fishing friend of mine, taught me the basis of this recipe and I have added bits and pieces to it. Since living in Christchurch, Izzy and I have become obsessed with catching salmon and any spare time we have we hit the Rakaia, Waimakariri, Hurunui and Waiau rivers. Salmon fishing is not easy and often we return home empty-handed but, when we do catch fish, this quick and easy recipe is super-delicious and can be used as an entrée or eaten on crackers for a starter. Note you will need a kitchen whizz to make this recipe.*

**PREPARATION TIME: 5 MINUTES • COOKING TIME: 15 MINUTES •
SERVES 4 (AS AN ENTRÉE OR 8+ AS A STARTER WITH CRACKERS)**

*400–500g tail end of salmon,
  de-boned but skin kept on*
*½ cup sundried tomatoes*
*1 sprig fresh rosemary, leaves
  only*
*½ cup fresh basil leaves*
*2 cloves garlic*
*¼ cup olive oil*
*salt and pepper*
*½ cup boiling water*

Preheat the oven to 180°C.

Place sundried tomatoes, rosemary leaves, basil, garlic, olive oil and salt and pepper in a kitchen whizz and blend together. The consistency should hold together nicely and be easy to spread like a paste.

Pour the boiling water into a small baking dish. Place a wire cooling rack down into it. Place the salmon on the rack and spread over the sundried tomato paste, ensuring you cover the whole salmon fairly thickly. Cover the whole dish with tinfoil and place in the oven to steam for about 15 minutes. (There is a fine line between undercooking and overcooking, so keep checking it. The salmon is cooked is when you notice the fat (white part) starting to push through and ooze out.)

When the salmon is cooked, either cut up and serve as an entrée or place the whole piece on a platter with some crackers.

# OKA (MARINATED RAW FISH)

*This delicious dish is so refreshing and a favourite in Samoan culture. Use a meaty white fish such as monkfish, so it holds up in the marinade, or hoki for a softer flake.*

PREPARATION TIME: 10 MINUTES • COOKING TIME: 15 MINUTES • SERVES 4

*4 monkfish fillets, cut into cubes*

*juice of 3 lemons*

*2 tomatoes, de-seeded*
*and diced*

*1 spring onion, finely sliced*

*1 small red onion, diced*

*275ml can coconut cream*

*salt and white pepper*

*1 teaspoon Tabasco sauce*

*iceberg lettuce leaves*

*half a red chilli, de-seeded and*
*finely sliced*

*coriander leaves*

*1 lime, sliced*

Put the fish in a bowl with the lemon juice and leave to 'cook' for 5–10 minutes. Add the tomato, spring onion and red onion to the fish and mix in the coconut cream. Season with salt and white pepper and add Tabasco to taste.

Line four small cups or dishes with lettuce leaves and fill with the fish mixture. Garnish with some chilli, coriander leaves and fresh lime slices.

Sunday rituals: market, food and family!

# FRITTO MISTO

*Deep-fried seafood . . . what's not to love?*

## PREPARATION TIME: 10 MINUTES • COOKING TIME: 5 MINUTES • SERVES 4

*200g fresh calamari tubes*

*½ cup milk*

*300g firm fish fillets*

*250g fresh or thawed prawns*

*¾ cup plain flour*

*¼ cup cornflour*

*salt and pepper*

*1 cup soda water*

*6 cloves garlic*

*1 litre canola oil*

*2 lemons, one finely sliced, one
    quartered*

*bag of baby rocket leaves*

*drizzle of olive oil*

*aïoli*

Clean the calamari well and soak in milk for a few minutes to soften it. Slice calamari into rings and cut the fish into bite-sized pieces. Dry all the seafood well with paper towels. Place flour, cornflour, and salt and pepper in a bowl and mix. Add soda water and stir to make a light batter.

Boil the garlic cloves in water for 4 minutes, before removing, drying well and slicing. Meanwhile, half fill a heavy pot with canola oil and heat on medium to high until it reaches 180°C on a thermometer. Have a bowl lined with paper towels ready.

Dip lemon and garlic slices in batter and, using a slotted spoon, drop them into the oil 5–6 pieces at a time. Turn and let cook for 1–2 minutes until golden. Dip the seafood in batter in similar-sized batches and cook in oil until golden.

Season again and serve immediately on a bed of rocket tossed with olive oil, with a bowl of aïoli and lemon wedges.

# SMOKED TROUT WITH GUACAMOLE

*Izzy and I love both fishing and camping more than most things in this world, and our absolute favourite place to do this is our summer holiday destination: Lake Waikaremoana, 'sea of rippling waters'. The two types of trout you can catch up there are rainbow and brown. Rainbows are by far the better-eating fish but browns are the trophy fish. The one I caught here from a fly rod was a 6-pound brown, which is great for smoking and eating on crackers! Note you'll need a fish smoker for this recipe.*

**PREPARATION TIME: 10 MINUTES • COOKING TIME: 15 MINUTES • SERVES 8+ (ON CRACKERS)**

1 brown or rainbow trout
1 teaspoon garlic salt
1 teaspoon Tuscan seasoning
1 teaspoon rock salt with chilli
   flakes
packet of crackers
Guacamole (see page 183)

methylated spirits
1 fish smoker
½ cup manuka sawdust

Gut, fillet and de-bone the trout keeping the skin on. Lay the trout fillets out, flesh-side up, and sprinkle with seasonings.

Pour methylated spirits into containers in the smoker. Place the manuka sawdust in the tray underneath. (This can be a very powerful fragrance, so half a cup is plenty.) Light methylated spirits carefully, place seasoned fish fillets on top of the smoker and cover with the lid. Cook for about 15 minutes.

Remove cooked trout fillets and place on a platter with crackers. Top each cracker with a scoop of freshly smoked trout and a dollop of guacamole. Perfection!

Our absolute favourite holiday destination: Lake Waikaremoana. With no phone service no power and no running water you can go back to enjoying the essentials in life: good food, good company and good times.

# PUFF PASTRY SQUARES

*A little bit retro but so simple to make and great for a light dinner or cocktail snack. Try the toppings I've given here — or get creative and create your own!*

PREPARATION TIME: 15 MINUTES • COOKING TIME: 25 MINUTES • MAKES 8

*2 sheets of frozen puff pastry*

## TOMATO & OLIVE SQUARES

*1 cup pitted Kalamata olives*

*handful of chopped Italian parsley*

*2 cloves garlic*

*1 tablespoon olive oil*

*1 teaspoon capers*

*juice of ½ a lemon*

*½ teaspoon cracked black pepper*

*sliced mozzarella ball or*
  *goats cheese*

*small punnet of cherry tomatoes, chopped*

*small bunch of thyme, chopped*

*handful of basil*

## SMOKED SALMON SQUARES

*1 cup crème fraîche*

*small handful of fresh dill, chopped*

*1 teaspoon capers, chopped*

*squeeze of lemon juice*

*dash of black pepper*

*white pepper and salt*

*1 free-range egg, beaten (for brushing pastry)*

*250g smoked salmon*

*small handful of fresh chives*

Preheat the oven to 180°C fanbake.

Cut each sheet of pastry into four squares. Gently score (don't cut right through) the edges of each pastry square with a knife, 1cm in, and prick the centres with a fork. Line two baking trays with baking paper. Lay out four pastry squares on each oven tray and place in the fridge to cool.

To make the olive tapenade (for the Tomato & Olive Squares), blend olives in a food processor with chopped parsley, garlic, olive oil, capers, lemon juice and pepper.

To make the herbed crème fraîche (for the Smoked Salmon Squares), simply mix crème fraîche with dill, capers and lemon juice. Season with salt and pepper.

Take the trays out of the fridge and, on one tray, prepare the Tomato & Olive Squares. Put a good dollop of olive tapenade in the centre and top with a slice of mozzarella, cherry tomatoes and a sprinkle of thyme. Season well.

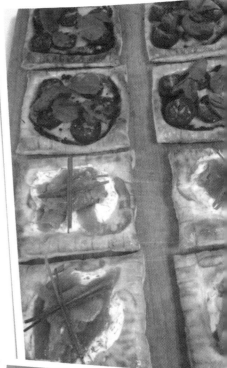

Bake for 15–20 minutes until golden and nicely puffed around the edges. Once cooked, garnish with fresh basil and add a dash of olive oil.

On the other tray, prepare the Smoked Salmon Squares. For these, we need to blind-bake the pastry so that the centres don't puff up. Line the middle of the pastry with a little baking paper (up to the scored line) and place rice or beans on the baking paper. Gently brush the pastry edges with beaten egg and bake for 25 minutes or until puffed and golden.

When cold, remove the rice or beans and line the squares with the crème fraîche mix. Top with smoked salmon and season well before garnishing with chopped chives.

# CHEESE & ONION SCONES

*Who doesn't love a good savoury scone? These ones are super-cheesy and all things delicious . . .*

**PREPARATION TIME: 10 MINUTES • COOKING TIME: 12–15 MINUTES • MAKES 8 LARGE SCONES**

*3 cups plain flour*

*6 teaspoons baking powder*

*¼ teaspoon salt*

*80g cold butter*

*1½ cups full-fat milk*

*2 cups grated tasty or strong cheddar cheese*

*1 small red onion, finely diced*

*½ teaspoon white pepper*

*½ teaspoon smoked paprika*

*2 free-range eggs, beaten, for topping*

*½ cup grated cheese, for topping*

Preheat the oven to 220°C, with the rack in the upper half of the oven.

Sift the flour, baking powder and salt into a bowl and grate the butter over. Using your fingers, gently massage the butter into the mix until it resembles fine breadcrumbs.

Add the milk with the cheese, red onion, white pepper and paprika. Using a knife, mix gently until just combined. Turn out onto a floured work surface and quickly form into a long rectangle. (The less you handle the dough, the better.)

Using a large floured knife, slice dough into 8 even-sized pieces and transfer them to a baking tray. Place close together but not quite touching. Brush the tops with the beaten egg before sprinkling with grated cheese.

Bake for 12–15 minutes until golden brown. Serve warm with butter and relish.

# ROASTED GARLIC HUMMUS

*Tasty, healthy and great with pita chips, this dip is easy to make at home. Just don't eat it on date night . . .*

PREPARATION TIME: 10 MINUTES • COOKING TIME: 1 HOUR FOR THE GARLIC • SERVES 6

*1 whole garlic bulb*

*½ cup tahini*

*½ cup lemon juice (about 4 lemons)*

*2 x 400g cans chickpeas, drained and rinsed*

*4 tablespoons olive oil*

*1 teaspoon ground cumin*

*2 tablespoons natural Greek yoghurt*

*salt and pepper to taste*

*olive oil, to drizzle*

*smoked paprika, to garnish*

*chopped Italian parsley, to garnish*

Preheat the oven to 190°C.

Cut the very top off the bulb of garlic and put in a tinfoil parcel with a little olive oil. Bake for 1 hour.

Whizz the tahini and lemon juice for a few minutes in a blender or food processor until it creates a creamy paste. The tahini should become thick and light in colour. This is the base for a lovely smooth and silky hummus.

Next add half the chickpeas, whizz for a few minutes, and then squeeze in four of the garlic cloves from the bulb, whizzing for another minute or so. Taste and add more garlic if desired. Add the remaining chickpeas, olive oil and cumin and process well. Lastly, add the yoghurt for that added creaminess, and season well before whizzing again.

Scoop out hummus into a serving bowl, drizzle with olive oil and sprinkle with paprika and parsley.

# ZUCCHINI FRIES

*So tasty, you forget you're eating vegetables! A healthier alternative to the classic potato fries, they're great for nibbling while watching the game with friends.*

PREPARATION TIME: 5 MINUTES • COOKING TIME: 20 MINUTES • SERVES 4

½ cup plain flour

1 teaspoon garlic salt

1 teaspoon ground black pepper

½ teaspoon smoked paprika

1½ cups panko breadcrumbs

½ cup finely grated Parmesan

2 free-range eggs

2 zucchinis

aïoli or relish, to serve

Preheat the oven to 200°C. Line a baking tray with baking paper and spray with a little oil.

Combine the flour with garlic salt, pepper and paprika and put on a flat dish. Mix the panko crumbs with the grated cheese and put on another flat dish. Whisk the eggs well and put in a small bowl.

Cut the ends off the zucchinis before cutting them in half and slicing into even-sized fries. Dip the fries into the flour mix, then the egg, before rolling in the breadcrumb mixture and placing on the baking tray.

Bake for 10 minutes before flipping and baking for a further 10 minutes, or until golden and crispy. Serve with aïoli or a nice relish for dipping.

# LEMON GARLIC ROAST CHICKEN WITH CREAMY GRAVY & CRISPY POTATOES

*This is a wonderful roast recipe made with just a few simple ingredients. For us, it always tastes best when the chicken is free-range. While I would usually cook my potatoes in the same pan as the chicken, cooking them separately makes them crisper.*

PREPARATION TIME: 10 MINUTES • COOKING TIME: 1 HOUR AND 15 MINUTES • SERVES 4

1.2kg free-range chicken

50g butter, softened

rock salt and pepper

3 lemons, quartered

few sprigs of rosemary

1 bulb of garlic, separated into
   cloves

good glug of olive oil

## GRAVY

300ml chicken stock

½ cup cream

cornflour, to thicken if necessary

## POTATOES

1kg Agria potatoes, peeled and
   cut into quarters

¼ cup olive oil

salt and pepper

30g butter, chopped

Preheat the oven to 220°C fanbake.

Unwrap the chicken, making sure the skin is dry before putting it into a roasting pan. Take a few good knobs of softened butter and, loosening the skin on the chicken breast, rub the butter under the skin into the meat for a few minutes. Rub the whole chicken with butter and season well with salt and pepper.

Fill the cavity with 4–6 lemon quarters, rosemary sprigs, and 4 cloves of garlic (skin on). Scatter the remaining lemon halves, garlic cloves and rosemary sprigs around and over the chicken. Season again and drizzle a good glug of olive oil over the bird. Set aside.

Roast the chicken for 20 minutes until golden and then turn the oven down to 180°C.

### RECIPE CONTINUED OVER PAGE . . .

# LEMON GARLIC ROAST CHICKEN WITH CREAMY GRAVY & CRISPY POTATOES

*(Continued)*

Cook for another 50 minutes, basting the chicken every 15 minutes with the pan juices, and squeezing out the lemon halves with tongs. To test whether the chicken is cooked, pierce the thigh with a knife. If the juices run clear (not pink), it is done. Cook for a further 10 minutes, if required.

Transfer the chicken to a plate and rest for 10 minutes, loosely covered in tinfoil, before serving.

To make the gravy, strain the pan juices through a sieve. Return the juices to the roasting pan and place on the stovetop on medium heat. Add chicken stock and cream, thickening with cornflour if necessary. Season well. You can sieve it again if you like your gravy extra-smooth.

For delicious crispy potatoes, have the oven at 220°C fanbake (you can put them in while the chicken is roasting). Boil a pot of water seasoned with a pinch of rock salt. Add potatoes and parboil for 10–12 minutes, until just soft on the outside. Drain and let sit for a minute with the lid on before giving the pot a good shake to roughen up the edges of the potatoes. Transfer them to a roasting dish with olive oil drizzled over and a good grind of salt and pepper. Cook for 25–30 minutes without turning. Add butter for the last 10 minutes of cooking time.

# SKINNY MAN'S BUTTER CHICKEN

*Butter chicken is definitely one of my favourite takeaway meals, but we all know that it's not very healthy. But, due to my love of butter chicken, I was determined to try and make a healthier version, replacing the usual cream and butter with coconut cream and unsweetened yoghurt. It still tastes amazing! Add in a nice raita (it can help douse the fire if a dish is a little too hot and spicy) and naan or roti bread for the full Indian experience.*

## PREPARATION TIME: 15 MINUTES • COOKING TIME: 15 MINUTES • SERVES 4

1½ cups rice

3 cups boiling water

½ onion, chopped

¼ cup tandoori paste

200ml chopped tomatoes (fresh or canned)

400ml can coconut cream

¼ cup chopped fresh coriander

½ cup chopped fresh spinach

1 tablespoon butter

1 cup plain unsweetened yoghurt

5 boneless, skinless chicken thigh cutlets

Raita (see page 184)

Roti (see page 188) or naan bread

Place rice and water in a rice cooker and leave to cook for about 15 minutes. If you do not have a rice cooker, then cook in a large pot on the stove, or in the microwave in a covered microwave-proof container, for 12–15 minutes.

In a large wok or frying pan, fry the onion over medium heat until slightly browned. Add the tandoori paste and mix. Add tomatoes, coconut cream, coriander, spinach, butter and yoghurt and simmer for 5 minutes.

Cut the chicken thighs into lengths or cubes and add to the sauce. Leave to simmer for about 20 minutes until the chicken is completely cooked through.

To serve, flip a ramekin of rice onto a large plate or bowl and scoop over the butter chicken. Top with a spoonful of raita and place a piece of roti or naan bread on the side.

# SPATCHCOCKED SPICED CHICKEN WITH JEWELLED COUSCOUS & RAITA

*This exotic chicken roast has a lovely aroma and is paired perfectly with a cooling yoghurt sauce. I also recommend serving it with couscous and a citrus salad.*

PREPARATION TIME: 15 MINUTES • COOKING TIME: 50–60 MINUTES • SERVES 4

### SPICED CHICKEN

1.5kg free-range chicken

1 teaspoon sweet paprika

½ teaspoon ground cumin

½ teaspoon ground cinnamon

¼ teaspoon ground ginger

¼ teaspoon cayenne pepper

½ teaspoon dried chilli flakes

4 cloves garlic, crushed

finely grated zest of 1 orange

2 tablespoons honey

2 tablespoons orange juice

1½ tablespoons olive oil

salt and black pepper

chopped fresh coriander, to
   garnish

### JEWELLED COUSCOUS

1 cup chicken stock

¼ cup water

1 cup couscous

1 tablespoon olive oil

½ cup chopped dates

¼ cup shelled pistachios

¼ red onion, finely sliced

handful of coriander

1 navel orange, segmented

*Raita (see page 184)*

Preheat the oven to 200°C.

To spatchcock the chicken, clean it well and place on a bread board, breast-side down. Trace your fingers down the back to locate the spine and, starting at the thigh, cut down both sides of the spine with a pair of chicken/kitchen scissors or your best knife. Discard the backbone and turn the chicken over. Press down on the chicken until it's nice and flat. Transfer to a roasting pan.

For the spice rub, combine the dry spices in a small bowl. Add the crushed garlic and orange zest, followed by the honey, orange juice and olive oil. Season with salt and pepper. Stir to make a paste.

Rub the chicken with the paste until it's completely coated. Place in the oven and cook for 45–50 minutes, basting with the pan juices every 15 minutes. To test whether the chicken is cooked, pierce the thigh with a knife. If the juices run clear (not pink), it is done. Pour the pan juices over the bird and leave to rest, under tinfoil, for about 10 minutes.

To make the couscous, boil the chicken stock and water in a small pot. Once it's boiling, remove from the heat and stir in the couscous. Leave to sit with the lid on for 10 minutes. Check to see if the liquid is fully absorbed (leave for another 1–2 minutes if not) before fluffing the couscous up with a fork. Add olive oil and stir through dates, pistachios, red onion, coriander and orange.

Garnish chicken with coriander leaves and serve with the couscous and raita.

Victor is a great kitchen assistant. Always present for the garnishing and eating!

# IZZY'S PRE-GAME TERIYAKI CHICKEN ON RICE

*This little beauty of a meal was taught to me by good friends of ours, the Robertsons. From when I first cooked it, it has become part of our weekly diet. Izzy refuses to have any other meal the night before his games. One of the most simple, tasty and oh-so-popular recipes we have stumbled upon!*

**PREPARATION TIME: 10 MINUTES • COOKING TIME: 15 MINUTES • SERVES 4**

*1½ cups rice*

*3 cups boiling water*

*5 boneless, skinless chicken thigh cutlets*

*400g Teriyaki Sauce (shop-bought or homemade, see page 181)*

*¼ cup sesame seeds*

*1 spring onion*

*4 cups coleslaw (shop-bought or homemade, see page 184)*

*2 tablespoons sesame seed dressing (shop-bought)*

*¼ cup Kewpie mayonnaise*

*avocado slices, to garnish*

Place rice and water in a rice cooker and leave to cook for about 15 minutes. If you do not have a rice cooker, then cook in a large pot on the stove, or in the microwave in a covered microwave-proof container, for 12–15 minutes.

Slice chicken thigh cutlets and add to the Teriyaki Sauce with the sesame seeds. Fold to mix.

Finely slice the green part of the spring onion. In a bowl, mix the coleslaw with the sesame seed dressing to coat it.

When the rice is nearly cooked, place the chicken and sauce in a frying pan on medium heat and cook for about 10 minutes. If the mixture gets too sticky, add some water and continue to cook until you have a nice smooth runny sauce.

To serve, scoop the rice into a small ramekin or bowl and flip onto a plate. Place chicken teriyaki over the top and the coleslaw mixture on the side of the plate. Sprinkle over the spring onion and place some avocado on the side. Drizzle mayonnaise over the top.

# VEGE-PACKED NACHOS

*Nachos are always a great rugby-night meal, especially for the kids. They are also a really great way to hide some veges in amongst all the other naughty ingredients. You can add any other seasonal veg you want, or replace the chicken with mince.*

**PREPARATION TIME: 10 MINUTES • COOKING TIME: 5 MINUTES • SERVES 6**

*4 boneless, skinless chicken breasts (or tenderloins)*

*1 onion, diced*

*olive oil*

*420g can chilli beans*

*500g tomato-based pasta sauce*

*2 tablespoons sweet chilli sauce*

*½ eggplant, finely diced*

*5 button mushrooms, diced*

*1 zucchini, finely diced*

*salt and pepper*

*corn chips*

*grated cheese (mozzarella is awesome)*

*½ cup Guacamole (see page 183)*

*½ cup sour cream*

*½ cup Salsa (see page 183)*

Cut chicken into pieces and place in a frying pan with the onion and some olive oil. Cook until onion has browned and the chicken is nearly cooked. Add beans, pasta sauce and sweet chilli sauce. Simmer on medium heat until the chicken is completely cooked.

Mix eggplant, mushrooms and zucchini through chicken mixture and cook for another couple of minutes. Add salt and pepper to taste.

Layer corn chips on six plates. Scoop nacho mixture over corn chips, dividing it evenly between each plate. Sprinkle over grated cheese. Place each plate under the grill until cheese is melted and chips are slightly brown. (They can burn super-fast so watch them closely!)

Allow the plates to cool a little, then add a heaped tablespoon each of Guacamole, sour cream and Salsa to each plate (or serve these on the side in bowls, so people can help themselves).

# CHICKEN & BASIL FILOS

*These little beauties are absolutely delicious, and a meal I often cook when guests come over. They take a little bit of preparing but are super-fast to cook. Izzy often asks for these filos, but they are not exactly the most highly nutritious meal so I like to save them for special occasions. Note a pastry brush will really help with this recipe.*

**PREPARATION TIME: 20 MINUTES • COOKING TIME: 10 MINUTES • SERVES 6**

6 boneless, skinless chicken
  thigh cutlets
1 cup olive or vegetable oil
1 onion, chopped
salt and pepper
3 zucchinis, grated
250g punnet sour cream
250g punnet cream cheese
135g tub basil and cashew pesto
375g packet filo pastry
¼ cup Parmesan
sweet chilli sauce, to serve

Preheat the oven to 180°C fanbake. Line an oven tray with tinfoil or baking paper.

Chop the chicken into small pieces and place in a frying pan on medium heat along with the onion and a little oil. Add salt and pepper to taste and fry the chicken and onion until chicken is completely cooked. Set aside to cool.

In a large bowl, mix together the zucchini, sour cream, cream cheese and pesto. Add cooled chicken and onion and mix together well.

Lay one sheet of filo pastry down (landscape direction) on a flat, dry surface. Dip pastry brush in oil and paint the corners, then paint an X in the middle and place another filo pastry sheet on the top. Repeat twice more. There should be four layers of pastry sheets. Cut in half with a sharp knife.

RECIPE CONTINUED OVER PAGE . . .

## CHICKEN
## & BASIL
## FILOS

*(Continued)*

Take one half and lay out in a landscape direction again. Place 4 tablespoons of the chicken mixture in the middle. Fold the bottom up and the top down, meeting in the middle. Then take the right end and roll and flip until you have a rectangle. Coat the open edge with oil to stick it down.

Repeat the process until all chicken mixture has been used up. You will usually get through a whole packet of filo pastry.

When all filos are lined up on the tray, sprinkle with Parmesan and bake for about 10 minutes. Watch them very closely; when the tops have a slight brown tinge they are ready.

Serve with a dollop of sweet chilli sauce and a yummy fresh salad.

# PORK BELLY IN A COCONUT, SAGE & GARLIC SAUCE

*Pork belly is by far the best cut of meat on a pig and, although none of us like to admit it, how good is crackling? With this recipe you will achieve both the crackliest crackling and the most succulent and scrumptious pork underneath. Pork is a meat that often goes very dry but, I assure you, there's nothing dry about this meal.*

**PREPARATION TIME: 5 MINUTES • COOKING TIME: 2 HOURS • SERVES 4**

1.3kg pork belly

salt and pepper

10 fresh sage leaves

2 tablespoons olive oil

400ml can coconut cream

4 cloves garlic, crushed

1 teaspoon cornflour

6 large potatoes

½ cup milk

2 tablespoons butter

½ red cabbage

2 teaspoons butter

2 tablespoons soy sauce

Preheat the oven to 240°C fanbake.

Pat pork belly skin dry with a paper towel and, with a sharp knife, score the skin down to the meat. Try not to cut the meat and make sure the cuts are close together.

Sprinkle the flesh side with salt and pepper, then place in a small roasting pan or baking dish on top of half the fresh sage leaves. Pour olive oil over the scored skin and sprinkle over a good amount of salt and pepper. Place in the oven and cook for 30 minutes or until the skin has achieved a brown, bubbled and blistered look.

When the crackling looks perfect, remove pork belly from the oven and add the coconut cream, garlic and the remaining sage leaves. The liquid should be covering all the flesh on the pork belly. If it is not covering it all, then find a smaller pan or dish or add another 200ml coconut cream. Turn the oven down to 180°C and cook the pork belly for another 1½ hours.

RECIPE CONTINUED OVER PAGE . . .

# PORK BELLY IN A COCONUT, SAGE & GARLIC SAUCE

*(Continued)*

With half an hour to go until the pork is cooked, peel and cut potatoes into small pieces. Boil the potatoes for about 15 minutes or until soft and breaking apart. Remove from the heat and drain. Add milk, butter and some salt and pepper and mash until smooth and creamy. Cover to keep hot.

Cut cabbage into slices, add to a frying pan with butter and soy sauce and cook for about 5 minutes or until cabbage wilts. Try not to overcook, as it tastes much better with a bit of crunch.

When pork is ready, remove from the oven and cut into squares on a chopping board. Because of the crackling, pork belly is quite hard to cut. Flip it upside-down, flesh-side up, and cut through.

To make the sauce, remove as much oil as possible from the cooking liquid that is left in the roasting pan. Place the liquid in a small pot with cornflour and cook for a couple of minutes until thick and creamy.

To serve, place a scoop of mash and a helping of cabbage side by side on a plate. Place pork belly on top and drizzle over the creamy sauce.

# STEAK WITH PEA PUREE, POTATOES & MUSHROOM SAUCE

*This meal is quite a fancy one and great for impressing when guests come over. It has a few elements to it, but they are all very simple and, when combined, create a magical dish. It is quite a heavy and substantial meal, so if making a dessert to enjoy afterwards make sure it's something light and fresh.*

PREPARATION TIME: 15 MINUTES • COOKING TIME: 20 MINUTES • SERVES 4

5 potatoes

olive oil

salt and pepper

500g steak or 1–2 steaks per
    person (either scotch fillet, eye
    fillet, sirloin or porterhouse)

## PEA PURÉE

1½ cups frozen peas

¼ onion, finely chopped

2 cloves garlic, crushed

¼ cup cream

1 tablespoon butter

## MUSHROOM SAUCE

1 onion, finely sliced

2 cloves garlic, crushed

1 tablespoon butter

10 button mushrooms, sliced

1 cup chicken stock

¼ cup crème fraîche or cream

RECIPE CONTINUED OVER PAGE . . .

# STEAK WITH PEA PURÉE, POTATOES & MUSHROOM SAUCE

*(Continued)*

Set oven to 180°C fanbake.

Slice potatoes about ½cm thick and place on a lined baking tray. Drizzle with olive oil, sprinkle with salt and pepper and cook for about 20 minutes.

For the pea purée, place frozen peas in a pot of boiling water and cook for a couple of minutes. Drain and return to medium heat. Quickly add onion, garlic, cream, butter and salt and pepper and cook for another 2 minutes. Remove from the heat and place in a kitchen whizz or blender and blend until completely smooth. If not quite smooth enough, push the purée through a sieve. Cover and keep hot.

To make the mushroom sauce, place onion, crushed garlic and butter in a frying pan. Fry until onion is browned, then add the mushrooms and let these brown a bit too. Add chicken stock and simmer for 15 minutes on medium heat, until the liquid has reduced and thickened. Add crème fraîche or cream and a sprinkle of salt and pepper. Keep on a low heat while you cook the steaks.

Coat steaks in salt and pepper and place in a hot frying pan with a little olive oil. Cook for 30 seconds on each side to begin with. Then cook for about 3 minutes on each side for a medium-rare steak. Leave to sit for a few minutes.

To serve, place a couple of scoops of pea purée in the centre of each plate. Cover with five or so slices of potato. Place the cooked steak on top and drizzle over the mushroom sauce.

# MEATBALLS IN HOMEMADE TOMATO SAUCE

*Italian inspired and heart-warmingly tasty, this easy dinner makes for tender and juicy meatballs. Serve over fresh pasta or with crusty ciabatta bread for dipping.*

PREPARATION TIME: 15 MINUTES • COOKING TIME: 30 MINUTES • SERVES 4

## MEATBALLS

4 slices soft white bread

1 free-range egg

400g lean beef mince

400g pork mince

salt and pepper

handful of finely chopped basil

2 tablespoons finely chopped
   Italian parsley

1 tablespoon finely chopped
   fresh oregano

½ cup grated Parmesan

1 teaspoon paprika

2 cloves garlic, minced

dash of milk (optional)

olive oil

## SAUCE

olive oil

1 large brown onion, finely
   chopped

2 cloves garlic, crushed

3 x 400ml cans chopped
   tomatoes

3 roma tomatoes, chopped

1 tablespoon tomato purée

1 tablespoon balsamic vinegar

salt and pepper

handful of torn basil, to garnish

grated Parmesan, to garnish

fresh pasta or crusty bread,
   to serve

RECIPE CONTINUED OVER PAGE . . .

# MEATBALLS
# IN HOMEMADE
# TOMATO SAUCE

*(Continued)*

To make the meatballs, pulse bread slices in a food processor until they are fine crumbs. Beat egg and set aside. Mix the meat together in a separate bowl, seasoning well with salt and pepper. Add the herbs along with the Parmesan, paprika and garlic. Combine the egg with the meat and breadcrumbs and add a dash of milk if more moisture is needed. Using your hands, gently roll the meat mixture into small balls. It should make about 12 large meatballs or 24 smaller ones.

Place meatballs in a hot pan with a little olive oil and sear the outsides, turning until an even brown colour. Set aside on a covered tray while you prepare the sauce.

To make the sauce, heat a little olive oil in a deep frying pan over medium heat. Add onion and sauté, moving frequently with a spoon so it doesn't burn. Once onion is nicely browned (about 6 minutes of cooking), add garlic and cook for another 30 seconds. Pour in the canned tomatoes, along with the fresh tomatoes, purée and balsamic vinegar. Season well with salt and pepper. Add the meatballs, turn the heat up, and heat until the sauce boils.

Once the sauce has reached boiling point, turn the heat down to low and cook the meatballs, uncovered, for 20–25 minutes, turning at the halfway point. Cook until they are no longer pink in the centre.

Serve in bowls garnished with basil and Parmesan, and either fresh pasta or crusty bread.

# MUM'S MEATLOAF

*This was an absolute favourite meal of mine growing up and is a family recipe that has been passed down. You can add any veges, herbs or spices to it that you want. Izzy loves to throw the leftovers in a sandwich the next day.*

**PREPARATION TIME: 10 MINUTES • COOKING TIME: 25 MINUTES • SERVES 4**

500g lean beef mince

450g sausage meat

½ cup fresh breadcrumbs

1 onion, chopped

1 teaspoon curry powder

1 teaspoon smoked paprika

1 cup chopped fresh spinach

½ cup chopped fresh parsley
    and basil

## GLAZE

¼ cup water

1 tablespoon Worcestershire
    sauce

1 tablespoon lemon juice

2 tablespoons brown sugar

¼ cup tomato sauce

1 tablespoon olive oil

1 tablespoon malt vinegar

2 teaspoons cornflour

Combine all meatloaf ingredients in a food processor and blend together. (If you do not have a food processor, use your hands.) Grease a microwave-proof baking dish and form the meat mixture into a loaf. Cover with a paper towel and microwave on high for 10 minutes.

Mix all glaze ingredients together in a bowl. Remove loaf from microwave and pour the glaze mixture over it. Microwave, uncovered, for a further 10 minutes. Several times during cooking, baste the meatloaf with the glaze from the baking dish.

Remove from the microwave, cover in tinfoil, and leave to sit for a further 5 minutes. Serve hot.

# IZZY'S MARINATED VENISON WITH FENNEL SALAD

*Hunting is one of Izzy's all-time favourite hobbies. He and my dad go out often; I tend to stay away. I always disliked the taste of venison until Izzy made this marinade to go with it. The marinade has a fairly intense flavour, so I have paired it with a nice fresh summer salad using one of my favourite combinations: fennel and avocado.*

**PREPARATION TIME: 15 MINUTES (MARINADE 2+ HOURS IN FRIDGE) •
COOKING TIME: 5 MINUTES • SERVES 4**

*4 venison steaks*

*olive oil*

## MARINADE

*2 cloves garlic, crushed*

*¼ cup soy sauce*

*4 tablespoons sweet chilli sauce*

*2 tablespoons olive oil*

*1 tablespoon Moroccan
    seasoning*

*salt and pepper*

## SALAD

*2 fennel bulbs*

*¼ red onion*

*1 avocado*

*1 orange, peeled*

*1 cup spinach leaves or rocket*

*juice of ½ lemon*

*dash of olive oil*

*sprinkle of rock salt*

To make the marinade, place the ingredients in a bowl and mix together. Add the meat, cover and refrigerate. If you have time, it is better to leave meat in the marinade for at least 2 hours.

For the salad, if you have a food processor or whizz with a thin slicing blade, then turn it on and put in the fennel bulbs and red onion. Or slice finely with a knife.

Cut the avocado and orange into thin slices and add to the salad along with the spinach or rocket, then drizzle over the lemon juice, olive oil and rock salt. Mix thoroughly.

Remove the marinating venison from the fridge. Place a dash of olive oil in a hot frying pan and add the meat. Cook for about 3 minutes on each side. (You can also cook this on a barbecue or hot plate.)

Leave to rest for a few minutes before serving.

**Note:** Venison continues to cook as it rests, so there is a very fine line between cooked and overcooked. Make sure you check often to ensure you don't overcook it.

# ROAST LAMB WITH ROSEMARY POTATOES & MEDITERRANEAN STACKS

*There are not many Kiwis who don't enjoy a good ole lamb roast. The typical lamb with mint sauce and roasted veges is usually found in most cookbooks, which is why I've made it a little different by adding a touch of the Mediterranean, with a dry rub and some beautiful vegetable stacks. Cold mutton sandwiches are Izzy's absolute favourite, so I make sure to keep any leftovers in the fridge for the next day.*

PREPARATION TIME: 20 MINUTES • COOKING TIME: 1½ HOURS • SERVES 6

2 tablespoons smoked paprika

2 tablespoons Cajun seasoning

2 tablespoons Tuscan seasoning

2kg lamb roast (preferably
    shoulder or leg, bone in)

2 cloves garlic

4 tablespoons olive oil


6 large potatoes

2 sprigs rosemary (leaves only)

sea salt and pepper

dash of olive oil

2 eggplants

1 tablespoon garlic and herb salt

olive oil

300ml jar roasted capsicums

400g feta

2 cups chopped basil leaves


Red Wine Jus (see page 182)

RECIPE CONTINUED OVER PAGE . . .

# ROAST LAMB WITH ROSEMARY POTATOES & MEDITERRANEAN STACKS

*(Continued)*

Preheat the oven to 180°C fanbake.

Mix together the smoked paprika, Cajun and Tuscan seasonings in the bottom of a roasting pan to make a dry rub. Sit the roast on top of the rub and roll around until the roast is completely covered. With a sharp knife, stab small holes in the lamb. Peel the garlic cloves and cut into small pieces. Push garlic pieces into the holes you've made in the roast. Lastly, pour olive oil over the roast and place in the oven, uncovered, to cook for 1½ hours. (You can also cook a roast on the barbecue, usually uncovered, for 1½–2 hours.)

While the roast is cooking, cut the potatoes into medium-sized pieces and place in a roasting pan lined with tinfoil or baking paper. Mix through the rosemary leaves, sea salt and pepper and olive oil. Place in the oven and cook for 45 minutes.

Cut the eggplant into 1½ cm thick slices and place on a flat oven tray. Sprinkle with garlic and herb salt and drizzle over some olive oil. Place in the oven and cook for 15 minutes or until softened.

Each of the eggplant slices will be different sizes. Start with the biggest slices at the bottom. Find the six biggest slices and place on a platter, then assemble stacks by layering with roast capsicum, feta and two basil leaves. Repeat again with the second-biggest eggplant slices, layering in the same way. Finish with the smallest eggplant circles on the top. This will give you six colourful Mediterranean stacks.

When the meat is cooked and carved, drizzle with Red Wine Jus. Serve the lamb, rosemary potatoes and Mediterranean stacks on platters on the table and let people help themselves.

# LAMB STEW WITH SCONE DUMPLINGS

*A great dinner for a cold wintry night, this stew uses an inexpensive cut of meat and can be left to cook in the slowcooker. A cheesy take on Jamie Oliver's scone dumplings are the perfect accompaniment to fill the puku!*

PREPARATION TIME: 30 MINUTES • COOKING TIME: 4 HOURS PLUS 40 MINUTES • SERVES 4

6–8 lamb neck chops

a few tablespoons plain flour

salt and pepper

olive oil

2 carrots, roughly chopped

2 celery sticks, roughly chopped

6 button mushrooms, roughly
  chopped

2 medium onions, finely chopped

3 cloves garlic, finely chopped

2 sprigs of fresh rosemary

500ml cabernet sauvignon

2 x 400ml cans chopped
  tomatoes

250ml cream

## DUMPLINGS

250g self-raising flour

125g very cold butter

salt and pepper

½ cup Parmesan

dash of milk

Toss the lamb neck chops in flour that has been seasoned with salt and pepper. Heat a glug of olive oil in a frying pan on high heat. Sear the chops for a few minutes until nicely browned. Set aside.

Cook the carrot, celery, mushrooms, onion and garlic in hot oil for 10 minutes. Transfer to the slowcooker. Add the lamb chops, rosemary, wine and tomatoes, and season well. Turn the slowcooker to low and cook for 4 hours.

To prepare the dumplings, place the flour in a bowl and grate the cold butter into it. Add a pinch of salt and pepper and rub the butter into the flour using your fingers until the mix resembles breadcrumbs. Add the Parmesan and a dash of milk to bring the mixture into a dough. Divide the dough into 8–12 even-sized dumplings.

Heat the oven to 190°C. Add the cream to the stew and sprinkle with extra seasoning, if needed. Carefully transfer the stew from the slowcooker to a casserole. Pick out any lamb bones if you wish. Place the dough dumplings in the stew, evenly spaced and only partially submerged. Put the lid on the casserole and cook for 30–40 minutes until the dumplings have puffed up slightly and are cooked through.

# SEAFOOD CHOWDER

*I got this recipe from my sister Sarah but have adapted it slightly. It is beautiful and creamy and, with a base of potatoes and zucchini, is not as rich as other chowder recipes. I usually use a fresh marinara mix from the supermarket, but you are most welcome to use any kaimoana that you love. Note you will need a slowcooker for this recipe.*

**PREPARATION TIME: 10 MINUTES • COOKING TIME: 5 HOURS • SERVES 4**

*3 zucchini, grated*

*2 large potatoes, peeled and cubed*

*1 cup cream*

*1 cup milk*

*2 cups seafood mix (e.g. calamari, fish, prawns, mussels)*

*1 cup fresh herbs (e.g. parsley, chives)*

*250g cream cheese*

*500g surimi*

*½ cup water*

*salt and pepper*

Place zucchini, potato, cream and milk in the slowcooker. Cook on High for 2 hours, then on Low for 1 hour.

Add seafood and herbs and continue to cook on Low for 30 minutes.

Finally, add cream cheese, surimi and water and cook on High for another 20 minutes. Add salt and pepper to taste.

Serve with some fresh garlic bread on the side.

# CRISPY-SKIN SALMON WITH BALSAMIC GLAZE & ORANGE KUMARA MASH

*Salmon is a household favourite and a great healthy fish to eat as it contains lots of good fats and omega 3. We love to serve ours simply with seasonal veg and delicious crispy skin.*

PREPARATION TIME: 10 MINUTES • COOKING TIME: 25 MINUTES • SERVES 4

4–6 orange kumara

a knob of fresh ginger

1 large tablespoon butter

salt and pepper

Balsamic Glaze (see page 183)

seasonal veges

4 salmon fillets, de-boned with
　skin on

2 tablespoons coconut or
　canola oil

Heat a large pot of salted water. Peel the kumara and chop into even chunks. Boil for 10–20 minutes, until soft. As the kumara cooks, make the glaze (see page 183).

Once the kumara is cooked, drain and add ginger and butter and plenty of salt and pepper. Mash well or use a stick blender. Set aside and keep warm while you cook the fish.

Prepare the salmon by patting down gently with paper towels until dry. (This is the key to crispy skin — you must remove all the excess moisture.) Season the flesh with salt and pepper. Heat a frying pan and add coconut or canola oil.

Gently rub the salmon skin with oil and place, skin-side down, in the pan. Set the timer for 4 minutes and, using a metal spatula, gently press on the fish for a few seconds to cook evenly. When the fish is ready, it should flip with little resistance. Turn gently and leave to cook for a further 2–3 minutes. Transfer to a plate, cover loosely with tinfoil and leave to rest for 4 minutes.

Steam the veges. Divide mash, salmon and veges between four plates. Drizzle the Balsamic Glaze on top or serve in a jug so friends and family can pour their own.

# STEAMED SALMON WITH ASIAN GREENS

*Steaming salmon is a great way to enjoy this rich fish, with the skin pan-fried separately for added crunch.*

**PREPARATION TIME: 10 MINUTES • COOKING TIME: 10–15 MINUTES • SERVES 4**

*4 salmon fillets*

*2 stalks lemongrass, trimmed into 10–15cm pieces*

*1 fresh red chilli, de-seeded and finely sliced*

*large knob of fresh ginger, grated*

*1 lemon or lime, sliced*

*¼ cup soy sauce*

*2 tablespoons fish sauce*

*1 tablespoon sesame oil*

*white pepper*

*2 bunches of gai lan (or broccoli)*

*2 zucchini*

*large handful of green beans*

*1 red chilli, de-seeded and finely chopped*

*2 cloves garlic, sliced*

*dash of soy sauce*

*sesame seeds*

*sliced spring onion, to garnish*

Preheat the oven to 200°C. Remove the skin from the salmon fillets with a sharp knife. Pat it dry with a paper towel and set aside. Make four rectangles of doubled-over tinfoil and place two pieces of lemongrass in each with a salmon fillet on top.

Scatter the chilli and ginger over top of the fish and place three slices of lemon or lime on top, squeezing some juice over. Combine the soy sauce, fish sauce and sesame oil in a bowl, then spoon this over the fillets. Season well with pepper before tightly folding up the tinfoil bundles: fold the sides over the top of the fish then tightly roll up the two ends. Cook in the oven for 10–15 minutes, depending on how you like your salmon.

While the salmon cooks, rinse the gai lan (or broccoli), finely slice the zucchini and remove the ends from the beans. Fry the chilli and garlic in a little oil in a hot pan. Add the beans, zucchini and gai lan with soy sauce and ¼ cup water. Put the lid on and steam for a few minutes. In a separate pan, cook the salmon skin in hot coconut oil until crispy. Season with salt and set aside.

Let the parcels cool for a minute or so after removing from the oven. Remove the fish using a fish slice, taking care to discard the lemongrass. Serve the salmon with the vegetables, scattered with sesame seeds. Garnish with sliced spring onion, if you wish.

# BEER BATTERED FISH & CHIPS

*This is a healthier version of that Kiwi favourite, the fish-and-chips meal. Our Homemade Slaw (see page 184) goes really well with this meal; and drizzle our homemade Tartare Sauce (see page 180) all over the fish.*

**PREPARATION TIME: 15 MINUTES • COOKING TIME: 45 MINUTES • SERVES 4**

*5 large potatoes*
*2 tablespoons chicken salt*
*2 tablespoons olive oil*

*2 free-range eggs*
*1½ cups flour*
*330ml bottle of beer*
*1kg thick white fish (e.g. hapuka, blue nose, bass)*
*2 tablespoons olive oil or butter*

Preheat the oven to 180°C fanbake. Line an oven tray with baking paper. Peel the potatoes and cut into chips, about 1½ cm thick. Lay potatoes out on the oven tray, sprinkle over the chicken salt and drizzle over olive oil. Shake and toss chips to make sure each chip is coated with oil and salt. Place in the oven and cook for about 45 minutes or until golden brown.

In a large bowl, lightly beat the eggs and add the flour and beer. Whisk together to form a nice thick batter. Make sure there are no bones in the fish fillets and cut each one into big chunks. Place all fish in the bowl of batter. Mix together to ensure each fillet is completely coated.

Heat a non-stick frying pan to medium heat and add olive oil or butter. Place 4 battered fish pieces into the frying pan at a time and let cook for about 5 minutes on each side. (The cooking time will vary according to the size and thickness of the fish. Watch and check during the cooking process to make sure you don't overcook the fish. If in doubt, gently slice through a fish fillet to check if cooked right through.) When cooked, place on a plate and cover with a paper towel to keep warm. Continue until all fillets are cooked, then serve straight away.

Sea fishing is another one of our favourite hobbies. In these photos we are catching hapuka and blue nose off the coast of Gizzy.

# BUTTERY FISH WITH LEMON SAUCE & GREEK SALAD

*Simply cooked fresh fish combined with a light tangy salad is perfect for a warm summer evening. Try this as an alternative to fish and chips and you won't be disappointed!*

**PREPARATION TIME: 15 MINUTES • COOK TIME: 10 MINUTES • SERVES 4**

## SALAD

*4 tomatoes, de-seeded
   and chopped*
*½ red onion, sliced*
*½ cucumber, peeled and diced*
*½ cup Kalamata olives*
*small handful of mint, chopped*
*125g feta, cubed*
*Balsamic Dressing (see page 182)*

## LEMON SAUCE

*½ cup olive oil*
*zest of 1 lemon*
*¼ cup lemon juice*
*1 teaspoon dried oregano*
*salt and black pepper*

*4 fish fillets (white fish, such as
   snapper), skin on*
*1 teaspoon canola oil*
*2 teaspoons butter*

To make the salad, combine all ingredients (except feta and dressing, which will be added just before serving) in a bowl.

To make the sauce, place all ingredients in a small jar and shake to combine.

Dry the skin of the fish well with paper towels. Brush the flesh of the fish with the sauce. Place oil and butter in a hot frying pan and add two fillets, skin-side down. Cook for about 3 minutes, until golden, and then flip and cook for a further 1–2 minutes. Transfer to a warmed plate. Repeat until all fish is cooked, changing the oil and butter for the second batch.

Serve the fish with the salad, which has had Balsamic Dressing drizzled over and feta cubes placed on top. Serve the lemon sauce in a small jug for guests to help themselves.

# PIZZAS

*The lovely pizza dough recipe on page 186 comes direct from my dad Roland, who runs gluten-free bakery Dovedale Bread. While they're not gluten free, they make for mighty fine pizzas. So have a go at making the pizza bases yourself or you can use shop-bought ones. Here are three of our favourite toppings . . .*

PREPARATION TIME: 30 MINUTES • COOKING TIME: 30 MINUTES • SERVES 6

It's hard to beat homemade pizza!

# GAMBRETTI (CHILLI PRAWNS)

*400g raw prawns*
*1 tablespoon olive oil*
*1 red chilli, finely chopped*
*3 cloves garlic, chopped*
*pizza sauce*
*1 cup grated Parmesan*
*1 lemon, halved*
*salt and pepper*
*handful of baby rocket leaves*

In a frying pan, sauté the prawns in olive oil and add the chilli and garlic, stirring until the prawns are mostly cooked through.

Spread pizza sauce on each pizza base, top with the prawns, Parmesan, and the juice from one lemon half, seasoning well, before cooking in a hot oven (about 230°C) for 12–15 minutes.

When the pizza is cooked, remove from the oven, garnish with a good handful of fresh rocket and top with the juice from the other lemon half and a drizzle of olive oil.

# ZUCCHINI, PROSCIUTTO & MOZZARELLA

*pizza sauce*
*2 zucchini, thinly sliced (use a mandolin, if you have one)*
*6 cherry tomatoes, cut in half*
*2 cloves garlic, peeled*
*small bunch of thyme*
*salt and pepper*
*250g prosciutto, cut into pieces*
*200g buffalo mozzarella, sliced*
*sprinkle of tasty cheese*

Cover the pizza bases with pizza sauce before layering with the sliced zucchini and cherry tomatoes. Crush the garlic cloves and sprinkle over the top with the thyme leaves. Season with salt and pepper. Add the prosciutto and finish off with the mozzarella and grated cheese. Cook in a hot oven (about 230°C), as above.

# THE CCC (CHICKEN, CRANBERRY & CAMEMBERT)

*½ cup cranberry sauce*
*300g smoked chicken meat*
*salt and pepper*
*½ red onion, finely sliced*
*250g camembert, sliced*
*½ cup grated mozzarella*

Spread cranberry sauce over the pizza bases. Cut up or shred the smoked chicken and arrange on top. Season well before scattering with red onion, camembert and mozzarella. Cook in a hot oven (about 230°C), as above.

KIWI PUDS

# BANOFFEE PIE

*This recipe is an easy 'cheat' version if you don't have time to make your own pastry and caramel from scratch. The combination of caramel, banana and cream is truly divine.*

PREPARATION TIME: 20 MINUTES • CHILL TIME: 2+ HOURS • SERVES 8

## BASE
*250g packet of digestive biscuits*
*4 tablespoons caster sugar*
*4 tablespoons cocoa*
*120g butter, melted*

## CARAMEL FILLING
*100g butter*
*100g brown sugar*
*395g can sweetened*
  *condensed milk*
*4 bananas, sliced*

## TOPPING
*500ml cream*
*2 tablespoons icing sugar, sifted*
*1 teaspoon vanilla essence*
*1 tablespoon Kahlúa*
*milk chocolate, grated (or 1 large*
  *crumbled Flake bar)*

Grease a 26cm loose-bottomed tart tin. To make the base, blend the biscuits, sugar and cocoa in a blender until it resembles very fine crumbs. Massage the melted butter into the crumb mixture. It should be pretty wet, so add more butter if it's too crumbly. Using your fingers, push the mixture into the bottom and sides of the tin, making sure it's evenly distributed. Cover and refrigerate for an hour.

To make the caramel filling, melt the butter and sugar in a pot over low heat until the sugar has dissolved and there is no longer a grainy texture, about 5 minutes. Add the condensed milk and increase the temperature until it boils. Stir vigorously for about 1 minute, then remove from the heat. (If any lumps have formed at the bottom, pour caramel through a sieve.)

Slice two of the bananas and fill the bottom of the tart with an overlapping layer. Pour the cooled caramel over the top, spreading into an even layer. Put the pie in the fridge for another hour to set.

Once set, gently remove the tart from the tin and transfer to a large serving plate. To make the topping, whip the cream gently with the icing sugar and vanilla essence. Be careful not to over-whip, the cream should be light and fluffy. Swirl through the Kahlúa.

To assemble, slice the remaining two bananas and push into the top of the caramel filling before spooning the topping into nice peaks on top of the tart. Sprinkle with chocolate shavings.

# DARK CHOCOLATE NUTELLA TART

*Nutella: the delicious hazelnut chocolate spread best eaten by the teaspoon! Or, to be a bit more civilised, in a tart.*

PREPARATION TIME: 45 MINUTES • COOKING TIME: 20 MINUTES • SERVES 8

frozen sweet short-crust pastry
    sheets or 1 batch of Sweet
    Short-crust Pastry (see
    page 185)
150ml cream
100g dark chocolate melts
¾ cup Nutella spread
2 free-range eggs, beaten
½ teaspoon vanilla essence
½ cup hazelnuts

Preheat the oven to 220°C and lightly grease a 15cm x 38cm rectangular tin.

Let the shop-bought or homemade pastry warm for a few minutes, then roll it out and cut a rectangle that overlaps the tin by a few centimetres. Gently press into the tart tin with your fingers and run a rolling pin along the edge to remove the excess. If the dough warms too quickly and comes apart, use your fingers to press large pieces into the tart case; making sure it's evenly distributed.

Prick the base of the tart with a fork and line the pastry with baking paper. Fill with baking beans or rice (to keep the sides from folding in). Bake blind for about 10 minutes. Reduce the oven temperature to 160°C, remove the beans and baking paper and bake for a further 5–8 minutes, until the colour deepens and the base hardens slightly.

RECIPE CONTINUED OVER PAGE . . .

## DARK CHOCOLATE NUTELLA TART

*(Continued)*

To make the filling, heat the cream in a pot until it is close to boiling point and bubbles have just formed around the edges. Remove from the heat, let it sit for 2 minutes and then stir in the chocolate, whipping together until silky and well combined. Stir through the Nutella and then whisk in the eggs and vanilla essence. Let it cool for a further few minutes before pouring into the tart case.

Bake for 18–20 minutes until set around the edges and only slightly wobbly in the centre. Let it cool in the tin before serving (or keep covered in the fridge for an hour or so).

To garnish, roast the hazelnuts on an oven tray for 5 or so minutes. Using a tea towel, rub the nuts gently to remove as much skin as possible. Lightly crush nuts using a rolling pin and set aside.

Decorate the cooled tart with hazelnuts. Serve with whipped cream and enjoy! This tart is also delicious topped with sliced strawberries or banana and dusted with icing sugar.

# LEMON & STRAWBERRY SHORTCAKE

*If you're in need of a fast, simple dessert, here is your answer. There is something wonderful about the combination of lemons and strawberries. You can also use other berries such as raspberries and blueberries.*

PREPARATION TIME: 10 MINUTES • COOKING TIME: 25 MINUTES • SERVES 4

1¼ cups self-raising flour

¼ cup white sugar

¼ teaspoon salt

1 free-range egg

¾ cup milk

1 tablespoon vanilla essence

zest and juice of ½ lemon

50g butter

1 punnet strawberries, sliced

2 cups cream

1 tablespoon vanilla essence

Preheat the oven to 180°C. Grease a 20cm round cake tin and line with baking paper.

In a bowl, mix the flour, sugar and salt together. In a separate bowl, lightly beat the egg and add the milk, vanilla essence, lemon zest and juice. Whisk to combine. Melt the butter and add to the egg mixture. Stir thoroughly.

Add wet ingredients to the bowl of dry ingredients and mix together. Stir in half of the strawberries.

Pour the mixture into the cake tin and bake for about 15 minutes. (It doesn't need too much cooking, so try not to let it brown on the top too much.) It's done when the cake springs back when pressed lightly in the centre. Leave the cake to cool for 5 minutes.

Whip the cream until thick. Add the vanilla essence and mix slightly to achieve a slightly marbled look.

Spread cream over the top of the cake and garnish with remaining strawberry slices. Alternatively, dust with icing sugar and serve strawberries and cream on the side.

# PEACH & BLUEBERRY TURNOVERS

*These little beauties can be filled with any seasonal fruit, but peach and blueberry go together nicely. If you're feeling adventurous, give the Cream Cheese Pastry a go or simply buy flaky butter puff pastry for very light parcels.*

PREPARATION TIME: 10 MINUTES • COOKING TIME: 15–20 MINUTES • MAKES 4

frozen butter puff pastry sheets or
1 batch of Cream Cheese Short-
crust Pastry (see page 185)
1½ peaches, sliced (or 410g can
sliced peaches, drained)
¾ cup blueberries (fresh or
frozen)
2 teaspoons cinnamon
½ teaspoon ground cloves
¼ cup soft brown sugar
1 vanilla pod, scraped (or ½
teaspoon vanilla paste)
1 tablespoon lemon juice
1 free-range egg, beaten, to
glaze
caster sugar, for dusting
icing sugar, for dusting
cinnamon, for dusting

Preheat the oven to 200°C for the Cream Cheese Pastry or 190°C if using butter puff pastry.

Slice the peaches. Combine peaches, blueberries, cinnamon, ground cloves, brown sugar, vanilla and lemon juice in a large bowl and mix gently.

Place the pastry on a benchtop lightly dusted with icing sugar. Divide the pastry into two, and roll each piece into a large flat rectangle. Using a side plate, mark and cut out two circles from each piece of pastry.

Place the pastry circles on a oven tray lined with baking paper. Put a quarter of the filling on one side of a pastry circle, leaving a 2cm border, and fold the other side over the top to create a half-moon shape. Pinch the pastry together to lock the fruit inside, and cut three slits on top with a knife. Repeat the process with the remaining three pastry circles.

Glaze the turnovers with the beaten egg and dust with a little caster sugar. Bake for 15–20 minutes until golden brown, then sprinkle with icing sugar and cinnamon. Serve hot with ice cream or thickened cream.

# TIRAMISU TRIFLE

*This decadent dessert has always been a much-requested favourite in the Dallas household. My dad Roland has handed down this well-guarded recipe so that you can enjoy it. Be careful, though! If it's not completely devoured, you'll be sneaking to the fridge at night . . .*

PREPARATION TIME: 30 MINUTES • COOKING TIME: 20 MINUTES
AND 2 HOURS CHILLING • SERVES 8

## ZABAIONE (EGG CUSTARD)
*4 free-range eggs, separated*
*75g caster sugar*
*450g mascarpone*

## SOAKING LIQUID
*1½ cups strong coffee*
*200ml Marsala*
*150ml Kahlúa or other coffee*
*    liqueur*

*1 Italian Sponge (see page 184)*
*    or 12 savoiardi biscuits*

## GARNISH
*good-quality cocoa*
*dark chocolate shavings*
*slivered almonds*

To make the zabaione, whisk 3 of the egg whites until stiff and shiny, about 3 minutes, and set aside. Whisk 4 yolks with the sugar, until the mix is pale and fluffy. Slowly add the mascarpone to the yolk mix and stir until well combined and there are no lumps. Fold the egg whites in very gently, keeping a light texture.

For the soaking liquid, brew a strong batch of coffee, cooling well, before mixing together with the Marsala and Kahlúa.

Slice the sponge in half and then cut each half into even-sized squares. Have a large glass dish ready, as well as the sponge (or savoiardi), zabaione and coffee mix. Quickly dip enough sponge squares in the liquid to line the bottom of the dish. Cover with a thick layer of the zabaione and follow with a dusting of cocoa powder. Continue this process for two more layers, ending with zabaione on top. Cover and refrigerate for at least 2 hours, ideally overnight.

To serve, dust the top with cocoa and garnish with shavings of dark chocolate and slivered almonds.

# MINI WHITE CHOCOLATE & RASPBERRY CHEESECAKES

*Baked in the New York style, these little beauties are great for a small after-dinner treat. The raspberry coulis cuts nicely through the sweetness, while the Krispie biscuit base adds a yummy coconut flavour.*

PREPARATION TIME: 20 MINUTES • COOKING TIME: 15–20 MINUTES •
MAKES 12 MINI CHEESECAKES

## BASE

¾ of a 250g packet of Krispie
   biscuits
100g butter, melted

## FILLING

120g white chocolate, chopped
375g traditional cream cheese,
   at room temperature
⅓ cup white sugar
1 tablespoon cornflour, sifted
1 teaspoon vanilla essence
2 free-range eggs, at room
   temperature
1 cup raspberries

## COULIS

½ cup caster sugar
3 tablespoons water
1½ cups raspberries
1 teaspoon framboise or rose petal syrup (optional)
zest of 1 lemon

Preheat the oven to 190°C and place paper liners in a 12-hole mini muffin or muffin tray (or two 6-hole tins).

Put the biscuits in a food processor and blitz until finely crumbed. Transfer biscuit crumbs to a bowl, add the butter and massage in with your fingers. Divide the biscuit mix evenly between the 12 holes of the muffin tray. Push the crumbs into the base of each hole with your fingers and compress well. Cover with plastic wrap and refrigerate for at least 30 minutes.

RECIPE CONTINUED OVER PAGE . . .

# MINI WHITE CHOCOLATE & RASPBERRY CHEESECAKES
*(Continued)*

Melt half of the chocolate in a bowl over simmering water on the stovetop (or in the microwave). Cool for a few minutes. Whip the cream cheese in a mixer with a paddle attachment until smooth. Add the sugar, a tablespoon at a time, until combined and fold in the cornflour. Stir in the vanilla and eggs, one at a time, folding in gently. Stir in the melted chocolate. Sprinkle the remaining chocolate and a few raspberries over the chilled bases and pour the filling mixture over the top.

Bake in the oven for 15–18 minutes or until the cheesecakes have risen. They may still be wobbly in the centre but will firm up once cool. Leave them to cool completely on a tray before refrigerating for 2 hours.

While the cheesecakes cool, make the coulis. Heat the sugar and water in a pot, over low to medium heat, for 3–5 minutes, stirring occasionally. Don't let the mixture bubble or caramelise. The sugar should be completely dissolved and the liquid a syrupy consistency.

Place the raspberries and sugar syrup in a blender and blend until well puréed. Push the purée through a fine-mesh sieve, to remove any seeds. It can take a while, so be patient! Stir in the framboise or rose petal syrup (if using) along with the lemon zest.

Carefully peel off the paper and serve the cheesecakes with the coulis spooned onto the top and decorated with fresh berries.

# APPLE & FEIJOA CRUMBLE

*This is such an amazing dessert and my dad's absolute favourite. It's a slight twist on the standard apple crumble. When feijoas are in season I often get lots and scoop them, bag them and freeze them, especially for this dessert. It makes a perfect mid-winter Kiwi pudding.*

PREPARATION TIME: 15 MINUTES • COOKING TIME: 45 MINUTES • SERVES 6

6 Granny Smith apples

10 feijoas

50ml hot water

## CRUMBLE

1½ cups rolled oats

¾ cup plain flour

½ cup brown sugar

½ cup shredded coconut

100 g butter

2 teaspoons ground cinnamon

Preheat the oven to 180°C fanbake and lightly grease an ovenproof baking dish.

Peel apples, cut into slices and arrange on the bottom of the baking dish. Cut feijoas in half and scoop halves into the dish. Pour in the hot water.

For the crumble, place the oats, flour, sugar and coconut in a large mixing bowl. Soften butter in the microwave, then add to dry ingredients and mix together with your hands until you get a nice crumble.

Scatter crumble over the fruit and spread evenly. Sprinkle cinnamon over the top.

Bake for about 45 minutes. If the crumble looks like it's browning too quickly, turn oven down to 150°C and continue to cook.

Serve with fresh cream and vanilla ice cream.

# CHOCOLATE SELF-SAUCING PUDDING

*This is one of my absolute favourite puddings! I have grown up making this pudding from a very early age. It is super-easy and a great way to introduce kids to the wonderful world of pudding making. It's one of Izzy's favourite puddings, too, so we could not get through winter without making this beauty at least twice.*

PREPARATION TIME: 10 MINUTES • COOKING TIME: 45 MINUTES • SERVES 6

*2 cups self-raising flour*

*1 cup caster sugar*

*3 tablespoons cocoa*

*⅛ teaspoon salt*

*100g butter*

*1 cup milk*

*1 free-range egg, lightly beaten*

*1 teaspoon vanilla essence*

*½ cup brown sugar*

*2 tablespoons cocoa powder*

*2 cups hot instant coffee*

Preheat the oven to 180°C and lightly grease a 1.5 litre baking dish with butter or oil.

In a bowl, mix together flour, caster sugar, cocoa and salt. In another bowl, melt the butter in the microwave and, when slightly cooled, beat in the milk, egg and vanilla essence.

Mix both wet and dry ingredients together thoroughly and spoon into the baking dish.

Sieve the brown sugar and cocoa over. Gently pour over the hot coffee. Bake for about 45 minutes.

Serve hot with freshly whipped cream.

Nothing like a choccy pudding to warm you up in winter. This is a true family favourite I had growing up and the first pudding I ever learnt to cook.

# BANANA CARAMEL PUDDING

*This gorgeous little pudding is so simple to make and is an absolute crowd-pleaser. Banana and caramel are two of my favourite flavours and, combined, create such a treat, especially in the winter months.*

PREPARATION TIME: 5 MINUTES • COOKING TIME: 45 MINUTES • SERVES 6

1 cup self-raising flour

½ cup brown sugar

3 bananas, mashed

¾ cup milk

75g butter, melted

2 free-range eggs, lightly
   whisked

1 teaspoon vanilla essence

½ cup caster sugar

4 tablespoons maple syrup

1 cup boiling water

Preheat the oven to 180°C and lightly grease a 1.5 litre baking dish with butter or oil.

In a bowl, mix together the flour and brown sugar. In another bowl, mix the bananas, milk, butter, eggs and vanilla essence. Make a small well in the flour and brown sugar mix and pour in the banana mixture. Mix all ingredients thoroughly.

Transfer the mixture to the baking dish. Sprinkle with caster sugar and drizzle with maple syrup. Carefully pour the boiling water over. Bake for about 45 minutes.

Serve hot with cream or ice cream.

# RICE PUDDING WITH BERRIES & PISTACHIO NUTS

*My dad always cooked us rice pudding when we were growing up. He did a microwave version, but this recipe is made in a rice cooker. (Rice cookers make life so much easier!) This is a great pudding with very simple ingredients. It's one of those 'oh no I have last-minute guests coming over and don't know what to make' kinds of pudding, as most of the ingredients should be in your pantry already.*

PREPARATION TIME: 5 MINUTES • COOKING TIME: 25 MINUTES • SERVES 4

1 cup rice

2½ cups water

400ml can coconut cream

1 cup cream

½ cup white sugar

2 bananas, sliced

½ cup raspberries

½ cup blueberries

¼ cup pistachio nuts, chopped

Place the rice and water in a rice cooker and cook for a full cycle. (It usually takes about 15 minutes until the rice is completely cooked.)

Add the coconut cream, ½ cup of cream and sugar and cook for a further 10 minutes, stirring often to stop the rice sticking to the bottom of the rice cooker. (After 10 minutes the pudding should be creamy and thick.)

Place a big scoop of rice pudding in each of four serving bowls and pour a little of the remaining cream over the top. Garnish with banana slices, berries and pistachio nuts.

Serve hot for dessert or place in a small container for kids' lunchboxes.

# AFGHANS

*These crunchy chocolate treats are Victor's favourites! Often requested for afternoon tea, the rich icing makes them especially decadent.*

PREPARATION TIME: 10 MINUTES • COOKING TIME: 15–18 MINUTES • MAKES 12 LARGE COOKIES

*350g room-temperature butter,
    cubed*
*1 cup caster sugar*
*½ cup cocoa*
*2½ cups plain flour*
*3 cups cornflakes*
*¼ cup chopped walnuts*

## CHOCOLATE GANACHE

*1 cup cream*
*400g dark chocolate melts*

*¼ cup whole walnuts*

Preheat the oven to 180°C and line a baking tray with baking paper.

Whip the butter in a mixer for 30 seconds until smooth, scraping down the sides. Gradually add the sugar until the mixture has doubled in size and is a light creamy yellow colour. (If the butter is too soft and the mixture is liquid, start again. It will cause the cookies to spread and be crispy.)

Sift the cocoa and flour, add to the butter mixture along with the cornflakes and chopped walnuts and mix briefly to combine.

Using a spoon, or your hands, press the mixture into round discs and place on the lined baking tray. Bake for 15–18 minutes. (They will still feel soft but will firm up as they cool, so be careful not to over-bake.)

While the afghans are baking, make the ganache. Heat the cream in a small pot over low to medium heat until almost boiling (bubbles will form at the edges) and then take off the heat. Add the chocolate. Let it sit for 1–2 minutes before beating together. Keep beating until glossy. Let it cool in the fridge for about 10 minutes before icing the biscuits.

Once the afghans have cooled, take the icing out of the fridge and stir well, before generously dolloping onto the biscuits. Garnish with a walnut on top and serve with a cuppa!

# BALLS OF GOODNESS

*Izzy said to me recently that he wants all the chocolate and 'bad stuff' removed from the pantry so he doesn't eat it. So I decided to try making some healthy snacks for him that are packed full of energy. This recipe is absolutely fantastic for an alternative snack for athletes, or can be awesome little energy balls to throw in the kids' lunchboxes. They are packed with goodness and are extremely simple to make, as long as you have a kitchen whizz. Feel free to add any other nuts or seeds that you like.*

PREPARATION TIME: 5 MINUTES • SETTING TIME: 30 MINUTES • MAKES 16–20

¼ cup sesame seeds

¼ cup sunflower seeds

¼ cup chia seeds

½ cup macadamia nuts

¼ cup sliced almonds

¼ cup LSC mix (linseed, sunflower and chia)

1 cup rolled oats

½ cup shredded coconut

2 tablespoons cocoa

2 tablespoons coconut oil

½ cup (3 heaped tablespoons) peanut butter

½ cup runny honey

¼ cup protein powder (optional)

Line an oven tray with baking paper.

Put all ingredients in a kitchen whizz and blend. You will see it is at the right consistency when the mixture forms large clumps. If the mixture is too dry and not coming together, add more honey and peanut butter.

When you feel you have the right consistency, roll tablespoonfuls into walnut-sized balls.

Place the balls on the lined baking tray and place in the fridge to set for 30 minutes.

Store in the fridge for up to a week.

# CARROT CUPCAKES WITH CREAM CHEESE ICING

*A great way to sneak some veges into the kids' baking! This yummy cupcake recipe is also perfect for the grown-ups' afternoon tea.*

PREPARATION TIME: 15 MINUTES • COOKING TIME: 18–20 MINUTES • MAKES 12 CUPCAKES

*1 cup wholemeal flour*

*1 cup self-raising flour*

*1 teaspoon baking powder*

*½ teaspoon baking soda*

*1 teaspoon ground cinnamon*

*1 teaspoon mixed spice*

*¼ teaspoon ground nutmeg*

*1 cup packed soft brown sugar*

*3 medium carrots*

*2 free-range eggs*

*150ml sunflower oil*

## ICING

*250g traditional cream cheese*

*1 cup sieved icing sugar*

*zest of 1 lemon*

*juice of ½ a lemon*

*1 teaspoon vanilla essence*

*handful of toasted walnuts, crushed*

Preheat oven to 160°C fanbake and line a 12-hole cupcake or muffin tray (or two 6-hole trays) with paper liners.

Place the wholemeal flour in a bowl, and sieve in the self-raising flour with the baking powder and baking soda. Add the spices and sugar and stir until well combined.

Peel and grate the carrots and set aside. Whisk the eggs with the oil and add to the dry ingredients with the carrot. Stir until combined.

Spoon the mixture into the muffin tray until each hole is three-quarters full. Bake for 18–20 minutes. Leave to cool on a rack.

For the icing, beat the cream cheese until there are no lumps and it's light and fluffy. Add the icing sugar, a tablespoon at a time, until well combined. Add the lemon zest and juice and vanilla essence and whip for a further few minutes.

Pipe or dollop icing liberally onto the cooled cupcakes. Roll the edges of the icing in crushed walnuts.

# BANANA & CHOCOLATE DROP MUFFINS

*These are Izzy's all-time favourite muffins. Sometimes he even heats a couple up in the microwave and adds cream for a yummy pudding. You can use chocolate chips, but I like to use chocolate drops as they hold their shape and don't melt, giving you that extra burst of chocolaty goodness.*

PREPARATION TIME: 10 MINUTES • COOKING TIME: 15 MINUTES • MAKES 12

2½ cups self-raising flour

1 cup caster sugar

¼ teaspoon salt

½ cup dark chocolate baking
   drops (or chocolate chips)

50g butter

2 free-range eggs, lightly beaten

¾ cup milk

1 tablespoon vanilla essence

3 large bananas, mashed

Preheat the oven to 180°C and grease a 12-hole muffin tray with butter or oil.

In a large bowl, mix together flour, sugar, salt and chocolate drops.

Melt the butter in a pot or microwave. Add the egg, milk and vanilla essence and stir.

Make a hole in the dry ingredients and slowly pour in wet mixture. Mix together but not completely, as this will make the mixture too runny. Add mashed banana and fold together.

Spoon the mixture into the muffin tray until each hole is three-quarters full. Bake for about 14 minutes. Remember: all ovens are different, so check the muffins and remove from the oven when lightly browned on top and when they spring back when pressed gently with your finger.

Leave to cool on a rack for a few minutes, then cut in half and add a sliver of butter while still hot, or heat a couple up in the microwave and add some cream for a scrummy pudding.

# MIXED BERRY & WHITE CHOCOLATE MUFFINS

*These muffins differ slightly from the old raspberry and white chocolate muffins, giving you bursts of all different kinds of berry flavours. If berries are in season, use fresh ones.*

PREPARATION TIME: 10 MINUTES • COOKING TIME: 15 MINUTES • MAKES 12 MUFFINS

2½ cups self-raising flour

1 cup caster sugar

2 free-range eggs

1 cup milk

1 tablespoon vanilla essence

50g butter, melted

100g white chocolate, chopped

1 cup mixed berries (frozen or
    fresh)

Preheat the oven to 180°C and grease a 12-hole muffin tray with butter or oil.

In a bowl, mix together the flour and sugar. In a separate bowl, lightly beat the eggs and add milk, vanilla essence and butter. Combine wet and dry ingredients and add the chocolate and berries. Mix together gently, being careful to keep the berries intact.

Spoon the mixture into the muffin tray until each hole is three-quarters full. Bake for about 15 minutes. Remember: everyone's oven is different, so check the muffins and remove from the oven when browned on top and not too soft to the touch.

Remove from the muffin tray and leave to cool on a baking rack. Serve slightly warm with a sliver of butter.

# PINK COCONUT & LEMONADE SCONES

*This classic scone recipe is a winner! It's soft and light — and just a little bit girly, with a touch of pink. It's bound to be a tea-party success.*

PREPARATION TIME: 5 MINUTES • COOKING TIME: 20–25 MINUTES • MAKES 8 LARGE SCONES

4 cups self-raising flour

¼ cup white sugar

½ teaspoon salt

½ cup desiccated coconut, plus
  2 tablespoons for garnishing

3–4 drops of pink food colouring

1 cup cream, plus a few
  tablespoons for glazing

1 cup lemonade, at room
  temperature

## CHANTILLY CREAM

300ml cream

2 tablespoons icing sugar

½ teaspoon vanilla essence

butter

jam

4 strawberries, sliced in half

Preheat the oven to 220°C. Line a baking sheet with baking paper and place in the oven to heat.

Sift flour into a large bowl and add the sugar, salt and coconut. Add food colouring to the cream and then add both the cream and lemonade to the dry mix. Using a butter knife, stir to make a soft dough with the pink swirled through, and then turn out onto a floured benchtop.

The less you handle the dough, the better the scones will be. Quickly shape the dough into a circle, about 2cm thick. Transfer to the heated baking tray and, using a blunt blade, cut into wedges. Don't worry if the sides are still touching, as you can pull it apart once baked. Glaze the top with a little extra cream and scatter over extra coconut.

Bake for 20–25 minutes, in the top quarter of the oven, until lightly browned and cooked through. Transfer to a cooling rack and cover with a clean damp tea towel (this will keep them spongy soft).

To make the Chantilly Cream, whip the cream with the icing sugar and vanilla.

Serve scones with butter, jam, Chantilly Cream and strawberries.

# TRIPLE CHOC PEANUT BUTTER BROWNIE

*If you love Snickers bars, then this is the brownie for you! It's rich and moist and goes great with an afternoon cuppa.*

PREPARATION TIME: 15 MINUTES • COOKING TIME: 25 MINUTES • MAKES 12 SLICES

*1 cup dark chocolate melts*

*1 cup milk chocolate melts*

*1 cup crunchy peanut butter*

*1 cup caster sugar*

*4 large free-range eggs*

*1 cup plain flour*

*½ cup cocoa powder*

*1 teaspoon vanilla essence*

## TOPPING

*¼ cup white chocolate melts*

*¼ cup dark chocolate melts*

*¼ cup milk chocolate melts*

*¼ cup salted peanuts*

Preheat the oven to 170°C. Line a 20cm square tin with baking paper.

Put dark chocolate and milk chocolate melts in a microwave-proof dish and gently melt, stirring every 30 seconds. Stir together with a metal spoon. You can also do this in a 'double boiler' (with the chocolate in a metal bowl set on top of a pot of simmering water). Stir through the peanut butter once the chocolate has cooled slightly.

Place the caster sugar in a bowl and add eggs one at a time. Beat, with a hand blender or mixer, until light and creamy (1–2 minutes on High). Fold the chocolate mixture into the egg mixture. Sift the flour and cocoa into a bowl, stirring to combine, and fold through your wet mix with the vanilla essence.

Pour the batter into the lined tin. Roughly chop the remaining white, dark and milk chocolate melts and scatter over the batter along with the peanuts, pushing them gently into the top.

Bake for 25 minutes, or until the mixture has crackled on top and is no longer liquid in the middle. Remove the baking paper with the brownie in it, and cool on a wire rack. Slice brownie and serve when cool, or store in a container in the fridge.

# PINEAPPLE LUMP, COCONUT & MACADAMIA SLICE

*I made this recipe up especially for Izzy, as his favourite lollies are pineapple lumps. I gave it a few trial runs using different ingredients, but this particular version was definitely the best. I once sent a batch off to the All Black boys in camp and it got demolished.*

PREPARATION TIME: 10 MINUTES • SETTING TIME: 2 HOURS • SERVES 10+

*250g packet malt biscuits*

*1 cup macadamia nuts*

*1 cup shredded coconut*

*70g Pineapple Lumps*

*120g butter*

*½ cup sugar*

*½ cup cocoa powder*

*2 free-range eggs*

*1 tablespoon vanilla essence*

Place malt biscuits in a kitchen whizz and blend until almost smooth. (Don't worry if there are still some bigger pieces, as this will add a nice texture.) Transfer to a large mixing bowl. Place macadamia nuts in kitchen whizz and blend until broken up, then add to biscuit crumbs. Add three-quarters of the shredded coconut, saving the rest for sprinkling on top.

Cut pineapple lumps into small pieces and add to the mixture.

In a pot, melt butter over a low heat and add sugar. Stir until dissolved and then add the cocoa. Mix together and remove from the heat.

In a small bowl, whisk eggs and vanilla essence together and add to the butter mixture. Beat together until smooth and add to the dry ingredients. Mix until well combined.

Line a baking sheet with baking paper, spread the mixture out evenly on top and flatten. Sprinkle over the rest of the shredded coconut, then place in the fridge to set for 2 hours.

Remove from the fridge and cut into small pieces.

>————(DD)————<

# TROPICANA CAKE

*I got the original version of this recipe from my sister Laura, who often makes it for family dinners. Although it is double-layered and looks quite fancy, it is probably the easiest cake I have ever made. You can either have it for a tea party or serve it with some cream for a dessert.*

PREPARATION TIME: 10 MINUTES • COOKING TIME: 45–55 MINUTES • SERVES 10

2½ cups self-raising flour

1½ cups white sugar

2 teaspoons baking soda

1 cup chopped macadamia nuts

1 cup shredded coconut (not
    desiccated)

2 free-range eggs, lightly beaten

2 x 440g cans crushed
    pineapple, juice and all

## CREAM CHEESE ICING

250g traditional cream cheese
    (at room temperature)

100g butter, softened

½ cup icing sugar

1 tablespoon vanilla essence

2 tablespoons passionfruit syrup

shredded coconut, to garnish

Preheat the oven to 180°C and grease two 20cm cake tins with butter or oil.

Place the flour, sugar, baking soda, macadamia nuts, coconut, egg and the pineapple in a large bowl, then stir thoroughly until combined.

Pour the mixture into the cake tins, dividing it evenly. Bake for 40 minutes. The cakes will be very moist, almost soggy on the bottom. But make sure they are cooked all the way through (when a skewer inserted into the centre of the cake comes out clean), so they don't collapse. Remove from the oven and leave overnight or until they are completely cool.

To make the icing, place the cream cheese, butter, icing sugar and vanilla essence in a kitchen whizz and blend until smooth.

Spread a layer of cream cheese icing over the top of one of the cakes and drizzle with passionfruit syrup. Gently place the other cake on top. Spread icing over the top of the cake and cover with more passionfruit syrup. Finish with a sprinkling of coconut.

# BEST BANANA CAKE EVER

*Banana cake with chocolate icing is my absolute favourite cake. I have tried many different recipes, and combined the best parts of some of the yummiest cakes I have eaten to create the Best Banana Cake Ever! It is easiest if you have a stand mixer for this recipe, but a whisk and a spoon work just as well.*

PREPARATION TIME: 10 MINUTES • COOKING TIME: 50 MINUTES
(PLUS 1–2 HOURS TO COOL) • SERVES 8+

*2 free-range eggs*

*1 cup caster sugar*

*150g butter, melted*

*4 large bananas, mashed*

*1 teaspoon baking soda*

*½ cup hot milk*

*150ml plain unsweetened yoghurt*

*2½ cups self-raising flour*

## CHOCOLATE ICING

*1½ cups icing sugar*

*50g butter, melted*

*2 tablespoons cocoa powder*

*2 tablespoons hot water*

*2 teaspoons vanilla essence*

Preheat the oven to 160°C and grease a 20cm high-sided spring-form cake tin with oil or butter and line bottom with baking paper.

Beat the eggs, sugar and melted butter in a small mixing bowl and place in the bowl of a stand mixer. Put the mixer on low speed and add in the banana, baking soda, hot milk and yoghurt. Add the flour and leave to mix for a minute or so, until combined thoroughly.

Pour cake mixture into the prepared tin and bake for 45–50 minutes or until the cake springs back when you touch it or the sides are pulling away from the edges. When cake is cooked, remove from the oven and allow to cool. Place in fridge for 1–2 hours.

While the cake is cooling, prepare the icing. In a bowl, mix together the icing sugar, butter, cocoa, hot water and vanilla essence until all ingredients are well combined. Place icing in the fridge to cool for 15 minutes.

When the cake has cooled, spread the icing evenly over the top. Either serve this beauty up for morning tea or add some fresh cream to it for a delicious pudding.

# CARAMELISED BANANA BREAD

*This tasty loaf is lined with sliced bananas to give it that extra intense flavour and a rustic appearance. Leave them out if you want a more traditional bread.*

PREPARATION TIME: 10 MINUTES • COOKING TIME: 50 MINUTES • MAKES 1 LARGE LOAF

*2 firm bananas*

*dusting of ground cinnamon*

*2 ripe bananas*

*1 teaspoon vanilla essence*

*150g butter (at room temperature)*

*1 cup firmly packed soft brown sugar*

*2 free-range eggs*

*1½ cups plain flour*

*1 teaspoon baking soda*

*½ teaspoon salt*

*½ teaspoon ground nutmeg*

*⅓ cup chopped walnuts*

Preheat the oven to 180°C and line a 23 x 12cm loaf tin with baking paper.

Slice the firm bananas into very thin slices lengthways. Carefully press the slices into the base and along the sides of the tin until the tin is completely covered. Dust with a little cinnamon and leave in the fridge to cool. Mash the ripe bananas in a bowl and mix with the vanilla essence. Set aside.

Using an electric mixer, beat the butter for 1 minute until softened. Slowly add the sugar and beat for a further 1–2 minutes. Turn the mixer off and transfer the batter to a bowl. Using a large spoon, beat in the eggs, one at a time, until well combined. Gently mix in the mashed bananas.

Sieve the flour, baking soda, salt and nutmeg together and fold into the wet mix with the walnuts.

Pour the batter into the loaf tin until two-thirds full. Bake for 1 hour. The outer bananas will caramelise to a dark colour, so check the centre with a skewer to make sure it is cooked. Remove the loaf from the tin and cool on a rack in the baking paper.

FROM
SCRATCH

# BASIL PESTO SAUCE
PREPARATION TIME: 5 MINUTES • MAKES 1½ CUPS

1 clove garlic

2 good handfuls of fresh basil
   leaves

4 tablespoons pine nuts

¼ cup Parmesan

juice of ½ lemon

¼ cup cream

¼ cup olive oil

Put all ingredients into a kitchen whizz and blend until smooth. If consistency is still too chunky or thick, add more cream or olive oil and continue to blend. Great for burgers, wraps, sandwiches, pastas and fish recipes.

# SATAY SAUCE
PREPARATION TIME: 5 MINUTES • MAKES 1 CUP

1 clove garlic, crushed

1 small piece of ginger, grated

2 tablespoons soy sauce

3 heaped tablespoons peanut
   butter (smooth or crunchy)

2 tablespoons honey

1 tablespoon sweet chilli sauce

¼ cup water

Add all ingredients to a pot on medium heat and stir to combine. Add more water if mixture is too thick. Great for homemade burgers or wraps, chicken skewers, stir-fries and pizzas.

# TARTARE SAUCE
PREPARATION TIME: 5 MINUTES • MAKES 1½ CUPS

1 cup whole-egg mayonnaise

¼ cup chopped gherkins

¼ onion

2 tablespoons lemon juice

salt and pepper

Blend all ingredients in a kitchen whizz or mix thoroughly in a small bowl. Great for any fish recipes and as a dipping sauce for seafood.

# TERIYAKI SAUCE

PREPARATION TIME: 25 MINUTES (15 MINUTES OF THIS IS LEAVING THE SAUCE TO REDUCE) • MAKES ABOUT 1½ CUPS

1 clove garlic, crushed

1 small piece of ginger, grated

2 teaspoons sesame seed oil

¼ cup brown sugar

150ml soy sauce

150ml mirin (Japanese sweet
   cooking wine)

½ cup hot water

2 teaspoons cornflour

2 tablespoons sesame seeds

Cook garlic and ginger in sesame seed oil in a non-stick frying pan on medium heat. When slightly browned, add the brown sugar and mix. Then add the soy sauce and mirin and let simmer for 5 minutes.

In a cup, mix together the hot water and cornflour and stir thoroughly, then add to the frying pan. Add sesame seeds and let simmer for 15 minutes, stirring occasionally to avoid sticking.

Great for teriyaki chicken, teriyaki salmon and stir-fries.

# CAPER MAYONNAISE

PREPARATION TIME: 15 MINUTES • MAKES 1 CUP

2 free-range egg yolks

1 teaspoon Dijon mustard

pinch of salt and pepper

2 teaspoons lemon juice

500ml olive oil

2 tablespoons chopped capers

zest of 1 lemon

small handful of Italian parsley

Using a hand whisk, whisk the egg yolks with the mustard, salt and pepper and lemon juice.

Very slowly dribble in the olive oil, only a few drops at a time, and whisk continuously until the mixture comes together. It should be creamy and not too runny.

Stir through the capers, lemon zest and parsley. Leave to rest at room temperature for an hour or two before refrigerating.

# MINT HONEY DRESSING

PREPARATION TIME: 3 MINUTES • MAKES ½ CUP (ENOUGH FOR TWO SALADS)

½ cup chopped mint

2 tablespoons olive oil

2 tablespoons liquid honey

juice of 1 large lemon

To make the dressing, simply mix the mint with the olive oil, honey and lemon.

# BALSAMIC DRESSING

PREPARATION TIME: 2 MINUTES • MAKES ¼ CUP (ENOUGH FOR ONE LARGE SALAD)

1 tablespoon balsamic vinegar

3 tablespoons olive oil

juice of ½ lemon

salt and black pepper

To make the dressing, place all ingredients in a small jar and shake to combine.

# RED WINE JUS

PREPARATION TIME: 10 MINUTES • MAKES 1 CUP

2 cloves garlic, crushed

1 tablespoon butter

1 cup red wine

½ cup soy sauce

1 tablespoon brown sugar

2 tablespoons sweet chilli sauce

½ cup water

salt and pepper

Cook crushed garlic in butter in a non-stick frying pan on medium heat for a couple of minutes until the garlic browns.

Add the red wine, soy sauce, brown sugar and sweet chilli sauce and stir together. Allow to simmer and reduce for 5 minutes.

Add water and salt and pepper to taste and cook for another 5 minutes or until a sauce-like consistency is achieved. Great for roast lamb, lamb racks, venison, steak and pork recipes.

# BALSAMIC GLAZE

PREPARATION TIME: 20 MINUTES • MAKES ½ CUP

1 cup balsamic vinegar

1 cinnamon stick

1 tablespoon soft brown sugar

Place balsamic vinegar in a small non-reactive pot. Add the cinnamon and sugar and bring to the boil. As soon as it starts boiling, turn down the heat and simmer gently for 15–18 minutes, stirring occasionally. Watch carefully as it can burn quite quickly. The glaze is ready when it coats the spoon and no longer has a strong acidic flavour. Remove from the heat and pour into a bowl to cool.

# GUACAMOLE

PREPARATION TIME: 5 MINUTES • MAKES 1½ CUPS

3 ripe avocadoes

3 tablespoons sour cream

2 tablespoons sweet chilli sauce

½ red chilli, de-seeded and
    chopped

squeeze of lemon juice

salt and pepper

Blend all ingredients together in a kitchen whizz, or mix by hand in a small bowl. Great for nachos, dips and burgers.

# SALSA

PREPARATION TIME: 5 MINUTES • MAKES 1 CUP

¼ cucumber

2 tomatoes

¼ red onion

½ red chilli

¼ cup Italian parsley

1 tablespoon balsamic vinegar

Chop cucumber, tomatoes and red onion into small pieces and place in a mixing bowl. De-seed chilli and finely chop. Roughly chop Italian parsley and add to bowl along with balsamic vinegar. Mix well. Great for nachos, dips and burgers.

# RAITA

PREPARATION TIME: 5 MINUTES • MAKES 2 CUPS

½ cucumber, peeled

2 cups Greek yoghurt

handful of mint leaves, chopped

pinch of salt

pinch of paprika

Cut cucumber in half and slice in half again lengthways. Remove the seeds with a teaspoon before finely dicing. Mix cucumber into the yoghurt with the mint, seasoning to taste with the salt and paprika.

# HOMEMADE SLAW

PREPARATION TIME: 10 MINUTES • SERVES 4 AS A SIDE DISH

2 cups shredded green cabbage

1 cup shredded red cabbage

1 carrot, grated

1 spring onion, finely sliced

1 tablespoon mayonnaise

1 tablespoon olive oil

1 tablespoon apple cider vinegar

poppy or chia seeds (optional)

Place cabbage, carrot and spring onion in a large mixing bowl. Mix mayonnaise, olive oil and cider vinegar together, add to shredded vegetables and stir through. Add seeds, if using. Great for teriyaki chicken or salmon, fish and chips, pulled pork sliders, and picnics.

# ITALIAN SPONGE

PREPARATION TIME: 40 MINUTES • MAKES ONE 20CM CAKE

4 free-range eggs

175g caster sugar

150g plain flour

50g cornflour

1 teaspoon baking powder

Preheat the oven to 180°C fanbake and line a 20cm cake tin with baking paper.

Beat the eggs for 10 minutes until light and fluffy. Slowly add the sugar and beat for another 5 minutes. Fold in the sifted flour, cornflour and baking powder and pour into the prepared tin. Bake for 20 minutes, until golden brown. Cool on a wire rack.

# SWEET SHORT-CRUST PASTRY

PREPARATION TIME: 30 MINUTES (20 MINUTES CHILLING TIME) • MAKES ONE 23CM TART CASE

*1½ cups plain flour*

*125g chilled butter, grated*

*⅓ cup caster sugar*

*1 free-range egg yolk*

*2–3 teaspoons cold water*

Combine flour, butter and sugar in a food processor until it looks like fine breadcrumbs. Add the egg yolk and water and mix until a dough just forms. Turn out onto a floured benchtop and knead with your hands until silky. Shape into a circle and wrap in baking paper. Refrigerate for 20 minutes before use.

# CREAM CHEESE SHORT-CRUST PASTRY

PREPARATION TIME: 40 MINUTES (30 MINUTES CHILLING TIME) • MAKES TWO 23CM TART CASES

*4 cups plain flour (400g)*

*½ cup icing sugar*

*200g cold butter, cubed*

*100g cream cheese*

*2 free-range egg yolks*

*4 tablespoons water*

Place the flour, icing sugar, butter and cream cheese into a food processor and process into tiny crumbs. Add the egg yolks and water and process until a soft dough has formed (it will ball up in the processor). Turn out onto a clean benchtop. Knead until silky and compress into a flat disc. Cover with plastic wrap and rest in the fridge for 30 minutes before using.

# PIZZA DOUGH

PREPARATION TIME: 1 HOUR 30 MINUTES • MAKES 6 PIZZA BASES

600g plain white flour

12g salt

9g dried instant yeast

400ml warm water

30ml good-quality olive oil

In a bowl, mix the flour, salt and dried yeast before adding water and mixing again until a dough is formed. Pour the olive oil in and combine before turning out onto a floured benchtop.

Knead the dough until it is silky smooth and quite elastic, at least 5 minutes. Depending on the flour strength, you may need to add a little more water. (If the dough breaks when stretched and is not elastic, add more water.) Divide immediately into 3 x 350g balls.

Leave the dough balls to rest for at least 1 hour in a warm place, covered with a clean tea towel.

Deflate the risen balls with the palm of your hand and roll out into large discs (5mm thickness is plenty). Prick rolled dough with a fork before adding toppings.

I cook my pizzas on a pizza stone to get a nice crispy base, but an oven tray lined with baking paper will do the trick too. Always cook pizzas on the highest heat until the crust is golden brown, about 12–15 minutes.

# FLATBREADS

PREPARATION TIME: 40 MINUTES • COOKING TIME: 20 MINUTES • MAKES 12 MINI FLAT BREADS

*2 cups self-raising flour*

*1 tablespoon sea salt*

*1 tablespoon baking powder*

*1½ cups natural Greek yoghurt*

*1 tablespoon runny honey*

*½ cup chopped Italian parsley,*
*plus extra for serving*

*olive oil or clarified butter, for*
*cooking*

Combine all ingredients (except parsley and cooking oil) in a food processor until a dough forms. Add a little more flour if it seems slightly sloppy. Place on a floured benchtop, knead into a flat round, sprinkle over the parsley, and then gently knead into a ball. Place in an oiled bowl, cover with a plate and set aside for about 20 minutes.

Put the dough ball on a floured benchtop and divide into two. Using your hands, roll each piece into a cylinder shape. Cut each roll into six even chunks. Using a rolling pin, roll the balls out flat until they are circular and about 3mm thick. Gently score each flatbread in the centre with a knife, to create 4–6 lines.

Heat a griddle pan on a high heat, add the oil or butter, and cook two flatbreads at a time, for 1–2 minutes on each side, or until they gently bubble and puff up. Serve immediately topped with a little butter and extra parsley.

Full credit goes to Jamie Oliver for the idea for this easy flatbread recipe. Super-simple to make and they taste great with homemade dips and stews.

# ROTI

PREPARATION TIME: 25 MINUTES • MAKES 8–10

2½ cups self-raising flour

¼ teaspoon salt

2 tablespoons vegetable oil

1 cup warm water

chopped fresh coriander and
garlic, optional

2 tablespoons butter or oil, for
cooking

melted butter, for brushing
over roti

Place flour and salt in a bowl and mix in the vegetable oil. Add the warm water slowly, gently stirring as you go until a dough starts to form. Add a little more water if dough is too dry, until dough forms a ball. Add chopped garlic and fresh coriander (if using).

Place the dough ball on a floured benchtop and knead, adding a little flour if the dough is too sticky. (Dough should be soft, but not sticky enough to stick to your hands or the benchtop.) Cover the dough with a damp cloth and leave to rest for 10 minutes.

Roll out dough in a large circle, about 0.5cm thick. Spread about 1 teaspoon of vegetable oil over the circle of dough, then roll the dough up into a long roll and cut it into 8–10 pieces.

Roll each piece out flat into a circle, about 15cm in diameter. Let dough rounds rest, covered with a clean damp cloth, for about 5 minutes.

Heat a non-stick frying pan to low to medium heat. Melt some butter or oil in the pan before frying the roti, one at a time, until puffed and lightly browned. Quickly flip to brown the other side. This should take about 45 seconds per side.

Once each roti has cooked, place it on a warm plate covered in tinfoil to keep warm. When ready to serve, brush each roti with a little melted butter.

Great with any type of curry.

# INDEX